Hyperreality

Hyperreality

How Our Tools Came To Control Us

FRANK MULDER

RESOURCE *Publications* · Eugene, Oregon

HYPERREALITY
How Our Tools Came To Control Us

Resource Publications
An Imprint of Wipf and Stock Publishers
199 W. 8th Ave., Suite 3
Eugene, OR 97401

www.wipfandstock.com

PAPERBACK ISBN: 978-1-7252-7790-8
HARDCOVER ISBN: 978-1-7252-7791-5
EBOOK ISBN: 978-1-7252-7792-2

AUGUST 6, 2021

Contents

Preface | 1

PART I: THE PROMISES OF HYPERREALITY

1 HYPERREALITY | 5
How an increasing part of our lives is lived in an artificial reality designed to make us feel satisfied and comfortable.

2 NEEDS AND DESIRES | 18
How consumer society is oriented towards fulfilling our desires, which, unfortunately, turn out to be insatiable.

3 HYPERRICH | 27
How the first promise of hyperreality, wealth through money, is not fulfilled, as money has its own agenda and behaves suspiciously like a religion.

4 HYPERSECURE | 40
How the second promise of hyperreality, security by control, is delivering in the short term but at the cost of expensive security systems that could turn against us.

5 HYPERCONNECTED | 53
How the third promise of hyperreality—belonging through status— has hidden costs and leads to a mass society that makes real belonging more difficult.

PART II: THE MACHINE

6 Powers Unleashed | 69
How the promises reinforce each other, how even sex becomes hyper-real, and how we can unleash forces without conscious choice.

7 The Technological System | 77
How technology has become an autonomous system with its own agenda, according to Jacques Ellul.

8 The Chicken Machine | 86
How the technological system leads us step by step towards more efficiency and homogeneity, in the direction of an impossible brave new world.

PART III: DAZZLING FREEDOM

9 On Ends and Means | 99
How Mahatma Gandhi restated the problem in terms of ends and means, which is ultimately a question of trust; or in other words, faith.

10 The Spirituality of the Way | 107
How we find a possible way out in the spirituality of Jesus, for whom the end does not justify the means, but vice versa.

11 Back to Reality | 113
How the good life is found in stubborn reality, in poor neighborhoods and dirty gardens, in the middle of the tears and joy of life in community.

Epilogue: Theology and Hope | 125

How this story translates in theological terms, and why we need apocalyptic thinking.

Bibliography | 135

Preface

THIS BOOK IS NOT the result of scientific research. Rather, it is a manifesto; an essay that got out of hand. I started it because I needed to write down what worries me, which is the conviction that I am increasingly kept busy by things that are not really valuable. By *things*, instead of people, nature, beauty, God, or anything else that makes life meaningful. Even more than that; I feel that everything meaningful is moving steadily out of reach.

As a freelance journalist I've talked to many people about this and I have written different articles about what I saw happening in economy, technology, politics, and religion. Some parts of this book have been published before in *De Groene Amsterdammer*, a Dutch weekly.

In the course of my research, I came across a concept that helped me to understand what is happening in our society: *hyperreality*. This word denotes an artificial reality: a reality meant to be a kind of improved version of the real thing. I think this concept, derived from philosophy, is a fitting metaphor for the slick and streamlined world we are currently building, where everything is planned optimally to make us satisfied, by catering, with the help of technology, to all our needs and desires: the need for economic well-being, security and social acceptance.

We could describe hyperreality as the showroom of the modern project of "progress": the promise that everybody can achieve happiness. I want to discover how this promise works exactly, and what mechanisms are used to fulfill it. I found out that these mechanisms do not deliver what they promise, but instead slowly undermine what we are actually looking for. This streamlined world is increasingly becoming a machine that is beyond our control. Indeed, it is controlling us: it needs us as cogs that have to keep on turning around efficiently. This is the central thesis of the first part of my book.

In the second part I zoom out a bit to analyze why technology, or *technique*, or the machine, should be at the core of our analysis when we want to understand this project of progress. For this I will turn to a French sociologist, Jacques Ellul, who described this phenomenon sixty years ago.

The last part of the book is more personal. The truth is that I do not believe that we can fix this problem with better organization, smarter technology or different politics. For me, it is a spiritual problem, so we will have to find a spiritual answer to it. We need a spirituality that can liberate us from our dependence on the machine. Juxtaposed with life in hyperreality, I will describe life in full reality. There, in the stubborn reality, in the mud, among people, among problems, we can find the truly good life, one that is much stronger and more beautiful and sustainable and life-giving than any machine.

I am not a native speaker, so I hope readers are not disturbed by my Dutch-English. I want to thank Leon Pauw and Paul Kingsnorth for their help in this translation and their corrections to my text. Kingsnorth is an English writer who has been writing for years already about the relationship between man and nature, between ideals and failure, and he comes to comparable conclusions as I do.

I hope my book may also inspire you to search for the good life in the midst of a broken world.

I

THE PROMISES OF HYPERREALITY

1

Hyperreality

How an increasing part of our lives is lived in an artificial reality designed to make us feel satisfied and comfortable.

DIAGONALLY BEHIND THE BUS driver, whom I passed with no more than an annoying beep from the scanner, a middle-aged woman is sitting, candy crushing on her phone. The driver looks bored, the radio is playing softly. He is driving a fixed route, hour after hour, with a small screen displaying the next stop and the correct arrival time, while the speaker emits an automatic female voice exactly informing the passengers about the next stop. The driver does not even glance at the incoming passengers, nor do they glance at him. They keep their eyes on the pass scanner next to him, which calculates to the cent how much must be subtracted from their account. While inserting my earphones to descend into my musical cocoon, I wonder if anyone would notice if one day the driver himself was replaced by a computer.

I: THE PROMISES OF HYPERREALITY

Technology has become our environment, our habitat. Often we do not realize how radically we are mechanizing our natural and social surroundings. In the cocoon of the music player on the bus, or in the cocoon of our acclimatized car, we travel to our work or our place of education, where we work under fluorescent light behind a screen and drink instant coffee not made by a coffee lady, but by a machine. With our eyes focused on the latest messages on our phone we walk through the shopping mall, with synthetic clothes being recommended by electronic beats and mannequins in shiny showrooms.

Our environment would be completely unrecognizable to our ancestors. Nature has been driven back. Sometimes, when the sky is clear, I take a few steps out of my door, out of a kind of ancient instinct to catch a glimpse of the Milky Way, but the only thing I see is the permanent twilight of the urban night glare. (When an earthquake knocked out the power supply in Los Angeles, in 1994, police got numerous phone calls from citizens worried about a "giant silvery cloud" over the city, which appeared to be the Milky Way.) I live by a square in a post-war neighborhood built from concrete. There is so much asphalt and stone, that even the birds keep their beaks shut. If I tell people about this, usually they look upon me with pity. But it is quite something that we have created neighborhoods where you do not see any stars twinkle or hear any bird whistle. The only thing that comes close is the soft whistle of an incoming text message.

The first time that this really struck me was when I returned from a poor country and set my feet on "developed" ground for the first time. As I was gliding on the long moving walkway at the airport, I was surrounded by walls, floors, gates and showrooms made of plastic, plate glass, aluminum and steel. Everything was artificial, everything was polished and smooth, everything smelled sterile. I had just come from a country where everything was crude. The streets stank, there was dust and dung everywhere, and the houses were made from stone or pieces of wood. In the market, there were carrots, onions, fruit, bags of flour and chunks of meat. In the supermarket here, you can find, in shining white shops with perfect lighting, twenty-three varieties of potato chip in carefully designed packages, on carefully filled shelves, consisting not only of potato and oil but also of ten other ingredients, mainly artificial. Of course, there are also carrots, but they are already cleaned, scraped, cut into pieces and prepackaged in cellophane.

This obviously colors our view of reality. To stay with these carrots for a while: when you always buy your food in the supermarket, you unconsciously start to think that all carrots are the same size and come out of the earth clean. That is why some people are disappointed when they see what kind of muddy, curved carrots I harvest in my vegetable garden. Maybe I would rather have the normal carrots, they then say. Those from the supermarket, the prepackaged ones; those are nice.[1]

This small example alone shows that technology does more than take over annoying tasks, like making coffee or washing clothes. Technology becomes our environment. It is the water we drink and the air we breathe. The devices create a world in which we can immerse ourselves, where we find our knowledge and shape our relationships, by watching the news, sharing family pictures on Facebook and WhatsApping with friends. For a recipe, we ask Google, and if we want to know how the economy is doing, we watch a talk show where economists play with growth figures produced by their computer programs. If our children are tired, we give them a screen showing movies suggested to them by an algorithm in a data center somewhere far off, and if we enter the bus, we pay with a device that is connected to a central computer that keeps track of where we check in and out.

This technical space becomes larger, deeper and more intense, and increasingly influences our lives. With our smartphone, we can communicate permanently with many people at the same time, and if we install the right apps, also with our thermostat,

1. Another titbit about those factory-scraped carrots: for each dollar you pay, the farmer gets a cent or two, which means that you pay more for the form than the substance. If you'd like to pay even more, you can also buy grated carrots—in my supermarket, they cost 8 euros for a kilo. This is expensive, though it saves you spending your time on grating, of course (and on buying chlorinated water, with which the carrot pieces are treated in the factory).

the lamps, and the baby monitor in the children's room. For many adults this is still optional, an add-on to their normal lives, but there is a new generation growing up for whom the cloud is what used to be the school hall. For a big part of the day, students are permanently living in a virtual reality. As soon as they wake up, they plug in into a conversation that has already started and that continues until deep into the night, sometimes in the form of an actual conversation but often also in the form of a game. It has become a virtual reality that forms a new layer on top of the tangible reality. That is why education reformers are trying to move more and more lessons to this new virtual space. According to my twelve-year-old son he hardly talks to his classmates during lunch breaks, since they turn on their phones as soon as they get the chance. When I asked him about this, he asked: "Why, what else can you do during the break?" "The same as what boys have done in the past few thousand years. Play cards. Play football. Or talk." He looked as if he couldn't imagine anything more stupid.

We often tend to think that this virtual space is fake, but that is not true. It is a real space that exists, where we relate and communicate. However, it is a space where we are separated from our immediate surroundings by screens. In a way we become detached people. Life in the technical biotope makes our relationship with natural reality lighter. We become increasingly distanced from the ground, the earth and the nature on which our whole economy is based. Our relationship with other people also becomes less tangible or physical, and more digital.

I am writing this chapter at a table in a nice coffeehouse. At the table next to me, a sixteen-year old girl is seated, together with her parents. They have not spoken to each other for the last fifteen minutes. The girl is bent over her tablet. She is finding herself in a space different from her father, who is playing with his mobile phone and might be checking the latest news, the weather forecast or his Angry Birds app. It is a space that is made from images. The mother looks out of the window, bored. It does not seem they are having a good time together. It does not seem they are even having

a together. They are together with others, in a space that you cannot feel when you are not logged in.

* * *

In the seventies, the French philosopher Jean Baudrillard coined
the word *hyperreality*.[2] It literally means over-reality. Hyperreality is a constructed world, a world made as a simulation and an
improvement of natural reality. It is not a fake reality. On the
contrary, it is *hyper*—more real than reality, in the sense that our
senses experience much more.[3]

Baudrillard did not know Instagram or Google, but he already recognized that modern society had become an image society. He saw that we are no longer people of words and stories, but
of images, design, photographs and movies. We have professors
in universities researching what designs or fonts or images best
convey a message to us in a leaflet or a website, and that is why
we are continuously bombarded by beautiful, well-constructed
images. An image is something artificial; that is to say, made by
people. That does not mean that it cannot refer to a real object. An
attractive Photoshopped picture of a cup of coffee on a billboard
refers to real coffee, the bittersweet taste of which you can feel in
your throat.

Yet in our society the image has slowly gotten its own life,
says Baudrillard. The real object to which an image refers is growing increasingly distant from the original. The Balinese beach on
the website is whiter than the original beach in Bali, and the poor
fishermen in their torn pants are edited out. That might seem like
trickery, but that is not entirely true, because in the meantime they
have constructed resorts that try to mimic the website and planted
palm trees on a white beach, to create the perfect tropical experience. (Believe it or not, but I have been to such a resort. I did not
see any Balinese there, of course. I met some, further down the

2. Baudrillard, *Simulacres et Simulation*.

3. I first read about the concept of hyperreality in a short book by an Australian youth pastor, Mark Sayers, *The trouble with Paris*. He puts a new spin
on Baudrillards' term.

beach, fishing between the rocks, one of whom even took me on the back of his scooter to show me his hut and give me some rice served on a banana leaf. I can imagine that nowadays the resort has built a few of these huts, to give all tourists the possibility of such an authentic experience, with guides wearing traditional clothes of course, and with precooked rice so nobody gets diarrhea, which I could not avoid back then, unfortunately.)

On the coffee billboard, meanwhile, we do not even see a cup of coffee anymore, only a nicely coiffed, nonchalant, and somewhat sarcastic-looking George Clooney. He still seems to drink coffee, but that is not essential. What the image refers to is more of a certain tasteful, self-conscious manliness than the liquid that we are to pour into our throats. Interestingly, the company that uses this advertisement does not really care whether this liquid is even coffee. Much more important is the sale of expensive cups and interesting flavors for people who find it important to have a streamlined kitchen and a shiny, aerodynamic coffee machine because they are tasteful, self-conscious people. That Clooney himself tells people that he does not even like coffee just adds to his aura of coolness.[4]

Advertising, of course, is just one example of a whole world of images that we have created that we call *media*. We tend to think that this media is a certain lens through which we see reality, but according to most philosophers, that is not the case. Media—literally, "the means"—have *become* reality. They have their own life, their own content, and sometimes they do not refer to anything original anymore but have become independent. That is what we in turn want to attune our lives to. Glossy magazines publish beautiful women on their front pages, and as a consequence women (and men) are comparing themselves to this image, and letting themselves be instructed as to what they regard as beautiful or not. People follow the media, instead of the other way around.

On TV and Netflix we watch different series about the social life of groups of young people in San Francisco, New York, or

4. I could not get proof of this statement about Clooney and coffee, but I am willing to believe it.

Amsterdam, who are beautiful and free, go out and party, have one night stands and are still really good friends afterwards. They live the life that deep down in our hearts we might like to live, too. I have not visited all these places, but I will still stake my claim that such a group does not exist in reality. Most groups of friends that I have met are not funny and handsome and rich and able to be "just friends" after they have had sex with each other. Besides, we know that the actors in these series, while they are usually rich, are also usually not too happy in love and not able to live their lives without worries either. Yet still, unconsciously, this influences our image of the "good life", compared to which our own life seems quite lousy.

Of course, social media also have an important influence on our idea of the good life. A friend of mine has 1831 friends, posts nice updates every day, and always gives smart reactions. She always shares nice jokes or videos, talks about her interesting job, and carelessly posts images of her enviable trips to Barcelona, Canada, the Gambia and Rome where she poses as a kind of photo model in front of the Taj Mahal, the Spanish Steps or other desirable locations with her just as desirable friend. Her life is ideal. At least it is on social media. I happen to know that in real life, she sometimes wishes to be dead. Obviously, that is something she would rather not post about. On social media, you construct your identity as you would like it to be, not as it is in reality. In reality, I might have a huge pimple on my nose, but I do not have any interest in putting that on display. And if everyone is doing the same—if all billions of profiles on Facebook are constructed the same way, and if that construction shapes the world that we go through and experience social interactions in—we need to be ask ourselves if the distance between society and tangible reality is growing ever larger.

You may think that my interpretation is too negative. With Facebook, you may say, you can get to know somebody from a country you would never have visited otherwise. And many of these technologies I am criticizing—well, they help us overcome restrictions and get much more out of our lives. But I am curious as to what it means that we are able to overcome ever more restrictions. Is it simply the case that we are unfolding and developing our potential?

Italian writer Umberto Eco would have denied this. According to him, we do not like the restrictions of tangible reality very much. Hyperreality is thus an attempt to improve it. The artificial reality we are creating has to look as real as possible, even more real than the real world. As Coca Cola puts it: what we make must be the real thing. Wise words, in a time of fake news, but even wiser if you realize that he wrote these words in 1975, in an essay called *Travels in Hyperreality*.[5] In this essay, he treats himself to a tour of wax museums. America does not have a lot of art history of its own and has therefore specialized in fake versions. The climax of hyperreality in these museums, according to Eco, is time and again the Last Supper of Da Vinci, made of wax statues. The original painting, printed in the leaflet, is nothing in comparison to the three-dimensional scene, with intense colors, sacred background music, and an automated voice-over explaining that this will be a once in a lifetime religious experience. When you leave, says Eco, you do not have to go to Italy anymore, since the voice-over has warned you that the original fresco is ruined and no longer has the power to move you as the three-dimensional wax; which after all is now more real.

The climax of hyperreality, according to Eco, is Disneyland, a place where fantasy has become reality and where the happy ending is available to everyone. Here, nobody tries to refer to an original at all. In Disneyland, fantasy is produced. The souvenirs here are not fake: they are original creations, like the fantasies themselves. After having experienced the Disney version of New Orleans and its wild water river, including artificial wild animals, Eco wanted to see the real Mississippi. But when the captain of the river paddle streamer tells you that it is possible to see alligators on the riverside, and yet you do not see any, you almost start to miss Disneyland, where the wild animals are readily available. "Disneyland tells us," writes Eco, "that technology can give us more reality than nature can."

5. Eco, *Travels in Hyperreality*, 43–44.

I could have given examples from our own times, but I found it more interesting to quote someone writing in 1975, because this shows that what is happening around us today is not unique to commercial TV or to Facebook or to virtual reality to present us a self-created reality. There is only one difference: as technology advances, it is becoming increasingly difficult to understand the difference between real and not real. That the ultimate goal is making money may be clear in a wax statue museum or in Disneyland, but not in *The Matrix*. In this movie, the people are kept in a kind of artificial womb, where their energy is tapped to fuel the computers, but their minds are completely immersed in a virtual reality. What they conceive of as reality, is just a projection. It is no coincidence that during one scene the main character, Neo, takes a book from a shelf about hyperreality, titled *Simulacra and Simulations*, written by none other than Jean Baudrillard.

* * *

Quite a few media philosophers argue that Baudrillard and Eco talk nonsense, and the makers of *The Matrix* even more. They reason that everything is projection, which makes it fundamentally impossible to differentiate between real and fake. Everything comes to us through images and impressions. We see a tree: our brains interpret their sense data as "tree", yet we will never be completely sure if this tree actually exists in reality. It could be a fake tree, or maybe we are drunk and think we see one. We only have impressions of reality, so these impressions become our reality.

Yet my common sense knows that though those philosophers may say this, we cannot escape the fact that some impressions are more authentic than others. Some images are more truthful. Our world is dominated more and more by images that are aligned to our desires; in other words, images that *feel nice*. This criterion I do not trust, because it paves the way for one-sidedness.

The Matrix portrays hyperreality as pure illusion, a false world, one which you must escape. I see it differently. It is not illusion, it is part of the real world, yet it is a reality that is consciously constructed to be "better" than the stubborn reality around us.

I: THE PROMISES OF HYPERREALITY

The hyperreal world wants to provide us with permanent comfort, ease, and satisfaction of our desires.

In this book, I interpret hyperreality in a broad sense. To me it is more than media. It is a helpful metaphor for what's happening in our technological society. There is a perfectly designed layer on top of the stubborn reality, liberating us from the boundaries of time and space. It has to be better and more real than the natural world. Women in magazines become thinner and more beautiful, thanks to Photoshop. Even the floor in our living room can be hyperreal, if we have artificial wood. It is much cheaper and easier to clean, and sometimes it gives an even woodier impression than natural wood. If I check the ingredients of the Hawaiian pizza that I am going to eat tonight, I find that the cheese is not real cheese, but fake cheese, made of palm oil. It is cheap, but still gives me the sensation of cheese![6] To get rid of the calories, I cycle. Not out in the rain, but in a climate controlled room with healthy fresh air at exactly the right temperature, where I can keep track of my heartbeat and other useful data. I can even choose to do this behind a screen with an inspiring landscape, since science points out that images of nature are still stimulating for our brains, something we inherited from our Paleolithic forefathers.

After my workout, I watch the news, with a live connection to a correspondent in Cape Town who explains something about the elections in Zimbabwe. Since Capetown is countless miles away from the events, his text is written by the editors in New York, but they need the correspondent for the personal touch.

And if I go out tonight, I meet a lot of good-looking men and women that all seem to be attractive, sexy, accomplished photo models. I have to admit that I often find this environment seductive. I want their attention, I want to belong with those interesting people celebrating their independence. But if I get out of this intoxication for a second, I realize that tomorrow morning they all look like normal mortal people who eat and work, have

6. For more information about fake cheese, check Wikipedia, which tells us that the stuff is called "cheese analogue" and was especially designed to melt well on pizza, while remaining chewy.

doubts about who they actually are, and wonder what on earth they should buy next to look just a bit like the beauties in the movies and the shop displays.

A big part of life in the city centers is hyperreal. There are real buildings and real people, of course, without masks. But we cannot escape the fact that everything is permeated by the myth of eternal youth and permanent fun. The shopping mall in my city has a slogan which is honest about its purpose: *fashion food freetime fun*. To the inventor of the indoor shopping center, the American Victor Gruen, a mall is not part of the city, but a new construction of the city itself.[7] Its purpose is to keep out the wild outside world, and its annoying aspects like beggars or cold wind, with the help of security personnel or air-conditioning, all to provide us with a frictionless, pleasant shopping experience. It is not a coincidence that a growing number of airports are taking up this mall concept, using the most advanced technologies to control the border and to track unwelcome migrants in a seemingly invisible manner, so as not to disturb the commercially attractive impression of limitless freedom.

* * *

I want to stress again that these examples are not bad in and of themselves. I only have to think of the valuable conversations I had in the hyperreal city with real friends while having real, tangible beer. If you look for it, it still is hardly possible to draw a distinction between good and bad or fake and real. An artificial additive to tomato sauce can help to conserve a real existing taste longer, and mascara can help to accentuate real beauty. But what worries me is that an ever growing part of our lives is becoming hyperreal. Philosophers will probably say that all technology is meant to improve reality, just as a bear's skin did in the past, so modern technology is in no way different and thus it is impossible to judge. That is nonsense. A quantitative change of something always leads to a qualitative change at a certain moment. It is not wrong to

---

7. Dijstelbloem, "Geruisloos landen," §9.

celebrate Christmas, but it would become a bit disturbing if we were having Christmas dinners 365 days a year.

There is no place for limits, discomfort or pain in hyperreality. If I look around me, on the square where I live, next to immigrants, single mothers and broken families, I see a lot of sadness. Unemployment, debts, dysfunctional religion, psychiatric problems, broken relationships. And me? It is hard for me to connect to them, because in the hyperreal world it is easier to live past each other. I work behind my screen most of the day, have virtual contact with like-minded people of my own social class, read posts of the people I like and buy cheap stuff from the other side of the planet (while my neighbor is sitting at home now since his computer shop has gone bankrupt). If I come home, I am too tired to socialize. And this is just about knowing the people in my neighborhood, let alone being touched by the poverty of the people who produce my stuff, for example, or who feel the consequences of our lifestyle through climate change. I know about it, but it does not sink in.

Moreover, I simply do not have time for that, because after work I have to cook, eat, do housekeeping, care for the children, read, read my email, do my administration, meet my friends, and work out. And besides all this I have to spend 14 minutes gaming, 99 minutes listening to the radio, 36 minutes browsing the internet, and 284 minutes behind my tablet or smartphone; at least, if I am an average adult, as calculated by researchers. All this only fits into one day if I multitask, which is quite stressful. I have only 8 minutes left for religion or spirituality and 8 minutes for volunteering. (And 308 minutes for television, of course, but that's the only way to relax after a day full of stress.)[8]

* * *

8. Figures refer to US adults, but they don't differ fundamentally from other Western countries. I took them from the American Time Use Survey 2019, carried out by the U.S. Bureau of Labor Statistics, and from media consumption research carried out by market research group Nielsen in 2020.

In a world that is oriented more and more towards the permanent satisfaction of our desires, we lose sight of certain aspects of reality that may be crucial. How can we connect to sadness, in ourselves or in others, if the whole world looks bright and happy? How can we care for nature, the fundamental basis of everything we build, if we have polished it out of our living environment? How can we connect to ourselves, if we are incessantly bombarded with contacts and images meant to amuse us and keep us distracted? I believe that the good life is more than merely satisfying instinctive stimuli.

Moreover, as a believer, I think that there is a God who speaks to people. But his is a whispering voice, that you can only hear if you become silent. You can also hear this voice through other people, especially outcasts. Some people hear this voice in the nature that we have been given, or in the historical stories of humanity. It is no accident that these are exactly the channels that we cannot tune in to anymore in a world that becomes more technical and hyperreal. Nature, history, the other, silence, suffering, all this is drowned out by an unending now that is searching for inputs to satisfy our senses and desires.

What kind of desires these are, and how they work, will be the subject of the next chapter. We will take a look at the ways or the routes that hyperreality offers us to satisfy those desires, and what kind of social mechanism this creates.

2

Needs and Desires

How consumer society is oriented towards fulfilling our desires, which unfortunately, turn out to be insatiable.

HYPERREALITY IS A WORLD of promises. The primary promise is the satisfaction of our desires. As humans we often don't feel complete. We miss something. We think that we will we happy if we find it. The object we miss can be abstract, like love or safety; but it can also just be a smartphone, the right scent, perfectly shaped hips or a freestanding house with a garden. This feeling of *missing something* is stronger in a secular culture, where we generally don't believe anymore in a spiritual goal for our lives. There is a void deep within us. Marketeers know this, and they use it. Drink this nice cup of coffee, they say, and the family warmth of old will return to you. Buy this Samsung Galaxy, and your life will be put in order; you'll save money too. Take out this mortgage; it will help to fulfill your dreams, and you can sit and relax with your beautiful partner on your white leather couch, happy and satisfied.

But we have arrived in a society where we already have everything. And yet still we feel this void. So we start to search, not for *things*, but for *experiences*. We long for the next experience. We long for the best massage, the most impressive concert, the best island, or for festivals offering all of this. We have become what economists call an *experience economy*. We are looking at our own lives more and more as a chain of experiences.

According to sociologists the satisfaction of our actual desires is slowly becoming a background reason for our continued consumption. Increasingly, we consume only to consume, buy only to buy, and travel only to travel. Not with a particular goal in mind, but merely to amuse ourselves. To keep ourselves busy, to distract ourselves, perhaps even to flee from an emptiness we all find deep inside. This is known as *hyperconsumerism*. As a consequence food, animals, even people, are treated as products we can take if we feel like. If we don't feel well, we start to eat, or to shop, or to watch a series, or a porn movie. We can get every impression or emotion we desire, without making any effort.

In his book on hyperreality, Australian pastor Mark Sayers writes that he often challenges people to spend the next weekend at home, unplugged, without books, friends, magazines, smartphones, computers, radio, TV, and other screens. Initially, most of them enjoy the space, but after a few hours boredom sets in.

> Come Saturday night most find themselves breaking down. One guy who got back to me after trying the challenge found himself, after twenty-four hours of no stimulation or distraction, sitting on his bed sobbing. In the quiet all kinds of pain from people's pasts emerge, and doubts about their worth invade the minds of otherwise confident people. Some find themselves almost paranoid, wondering what their friends are doing and whether they are having fun without them[1]

When you experience these feelings, Sayers says, you really start to understand how hyperreality acts as a smoke screen,

---

1. Sayers, *The Trouble With Paris*, 83.

distracting us from the causes of our unhappiness. He cites the Catholic author Henri Nouwen:

> Our culture has become incredibly ingenious at evading pain. Not just physical pain, but also emotional and mental pain. If we do not have a project to finish, a friend to visit, a book to read, no television to watch, and we are left to ourselves, we are confronted with the deepest sense of loneliness, and we become so afraid of feeling it, that we will do anything to occupy ourselves again and continue the play that promises us that everything is fine.[2]

But if we numb ourselves we mostly live in the present, and do not have the mental space to think ahead, or even backwards. In a world where media continuously demands our attention, this has become the new normal. Youth tends to be quite honest in this regard. In surveys on social media, young people will point to the fact they cannot go without distraction, or that they feel lonely if they read a book. Social media enables young people that are focused on groups and maintaining contact with friends, to be in constant connection with anyone and anything. Whereas emails have a beginning and an end, Twitter and WhatsApp conversations go on and on, whether you are participating or not. All of life takes place in the *now*: a stretched-out now without beginning or end.

You do not have to be a cultural pessimist to see that as a result of this process we have become more disconnected from our surroundings. It is very hard to truly contemplate the factory where our fashion is produced, or how reality TV is made, or what a sarcastic Twitter user actually feels. Everything in this milieu is about the experience, the immediate sensation. This means that we increasingly live our lives on the surface of things. When we plan our trips to Thailand or Guatemala, we make sure to book the most exciting all-inclusive jungle hike because we do not want to miss out on anything, but we have no interest in the banality and

2. Henri Nouwen, *Reaching Out*, as quoted in Sayers, *The Trouble With Paris*, 84.

hardship of everyday life in those places. Even the news is subjected to this process, as it has to fit within simple headlines and bite-sized videos, while nuance and facts are replaced by flashy clickbait. Politicians fill the air with catchy oneliners or even hateful attacks against opponents since they know the audience wants spectacle, not arguments.

Obviously, this does not only apply to lower social classes. Talk shows catering for a more highly-educated audience are just as deliberately designed to amuse people. I may claim that I find these shows informative, but in all honesty I watch them because I am entertained by their flashy videos, spry guests and their easy to consume analysis of the world. Boring gray-haired elderly people might be more interesting, wiser even, but they do not make it onto the show. The world of these TV programs, the world of the inner cities, of shop windows, of hyperreality, is not inhabited by such people. In this world, everyone is eternally young, dynamic, and charming. This is why it is so appealing! And yet the end result is that I lose connection to all that is not dynamic; whether it be elderly people, the imperfect carrots from my yard, or the literature of the people that work on the assembly line every day to produce our dynamic products.

Still, it feels good.

* * *

I want to dwell on these desires for a moment. They sit at the heart of our postmodern culture. Only when we determine our own desires are we truly free. We are supposed to enjoy life to the fullest, fire up our passions, and strive towards our dream job and our perfect partner(s). Only when we listen to our deepest desires will we live an authentic life. But can we actually trust our desires?

Psychologists have come up with the excellent term *miswanting*. By this they mean that we often desire things that do not actually make us happy. An example is spare time. We all want to be free, yet psychological research indicates that people feel more fulfilled when they are at work. This seems odd, since spare time is supposed to be the greatest thing in the world. Apparently, it is not. People tend to feel more positive when they lose themselves in the flow of a difficult challenge. However, it is a social convention that being free is better than working, which makes us desire the wrong thing.[3]

Equally misleading is our desire for as much choice as possible. As an example I can think of my own holiday planning. I want to travel to a place where there is plenty to experience, where I will be free to move, and where I can hike through rugged nature just as easy as I can visit picturesque villages and authentic restaurants. And of course I will need a car so I will be able to do all these things within a week or two. I do not want to miss a thing. But if I am honest, I think these holidays are also the ones that satisfy me the least. I am too occupied with optimization, driving around from one place to the other, in search of the most authentic place. My happiest holidays were those where we stayed in one place, forced to make the best of what we had. The ones where we took the kids to play at the imperfect creek, and to eat at a snack bar draped in fluorescent light where the fries were too oily. In short, I too cannot trust that my desires are truly aimed at that which I really think would be good for me.

Our desires are still more fundamentally flawed than this, though. René Girard, a French social scientist, demonstrated this with his theory of the "mimetic desire". His argument is quite simple, yet very compelling. As he puts it, we often believe that our desires stem from within ourselves, and that our choice of what to desire is our own as long as we remain true to ourselves. This, however, is an illusion. In fact, it is a "romantic lie". Rather than autonomous, independent creatures, we are at our core mere copy-cats who simply want what others have. Our desires are "mimetic", Girard explains. Mimesis means imitation. People will always want to copy and compete with one another. This starts during childhood. Even if there are hundreds of toys to choose from, a child will want the one toy another child is playing with. In adult life, that one toy will have changed into other people's cars, houses, husbands and wives. That is how humans and their desires are

---

3. I learned about miswanting from Carr, *Glass Cage*.

biologically wired. We might not be able to change this, but we can learn to understand it.[4]

Read Dostoevsky, for example. All his novels revolve around men who passionately desire a complex woman who seems to be close to the glamorous new guy in town whom they regard both as best friend and deadly rival. Usually there's also an ex-lover in the game who needs to be impressed by one of them. Yet sooner or later the rival loses his interest in the lady and the passion of the main character, too, goes up in smoke, leaving everything behind in shatters.

These are not just nice stories, Girard says. Dostoevsky has actual insight into human nature, much like other great novelists. They see what the romantic social scientists of the twentieth century have not been able to see: we do not desire autonomously; we want to have what the other has. We desire through the other, so to speak. We want to imitate the other, in fact, but we also want to be imitated, because we long for the other's desire.

Of course, I can single out Dostoevsky's jealous characters, or children fighting over the same toy, but I am no different to them. Why do I suddenly want to wear lumberjack shirts this season, while I threw out most of them only a few years ago? Why did I start drinking wine instead of beer now that I am older? Why did I buy Crocs, those unsightly clogs? Because the people I admire bought Crocs. I desire what they desire. And they desire my desire, as Girard would say. They want followers, and I want acknowledgment.

I am fibbing a little bit here, since I, an original and independent human, would never fall for such silly looking footwear. Obviously, I buy a more original alternative. Yet, even by not wanting to copy others I am copying. I want to prove that I am one of those people who go their own way, regardless of commercialized trends, and have their own unique style. People like us meet in

---

4. If you want to know more about the thought of René Girard, it's best to read his book *Things Hidden Since the Foundation of the World*. After reading this book the world will never be the same; you will discover mimetic desire and scapegoats all around you.

stores where we buy incredibly expensive shoes, fashioned in a vintage style to make them look authentically secondhand. And so we all feel unique, together. But in reality we are not unique, and our fashion is not just a matter of taste. The shopping mall is the arena where we fight for status and rivalry and recognition. Show me your clothes and I will tell you where you are in the hierarchy.

To cut a long story short: this mechanism is inescapable. Ultimately it is not about the stuff, it is about the other. It is the other and their desires we want to imitate. This makes our desires dynamic. They develop along with what we already have, and what our examples and rivals have. This is not necessarily bad. After all, it is how we are wired, and it helps us to learn when we are newborn. It does, however, help to realize that externalities will never be able to satisfy our inner desires, and that they will never be able to fill the void that is within us all. As soon as it is filled, the void grows again.

* * *

In the past, our desires were restricted, both because resources were limited and because people believed there were more important aspects to life. It was important to stick to the norms of your social class; to transgress them was inappropriate. But this does not mean that our desires are of themselves wrong. They are dynamic, and they often deceive us, but behind our mimetic desires are human needs. A few things are essential for humans to live and develop.

In the previous century, psychologist Abraham Maslow came up with his famous pyramid to show which of these needs must be met before we can focus on the higher goal of self-development. First and foremost, he argued, the basic needs are physiological: needs like food, drink, and clothing. Next in the hierarchy comes safety and security, followed by the need for social contact. Indeed, we are only human when we feel a sense of belonging. Only then will we be able to develop and flourish.

Our desires are situated in the same domain as our needs. They are: material comfort (which I understand more broadly as wealth), security, and belonging. I will take these three as starting point for the remainder of this book. We cannot live without them, yet they are also treacherous, since often we are not exactly aware of what we truly need and what we are made to believe we need.

Note that each of our desires is accompanied by a certain inner fear. We are afraid to fall short, afraid of a lack of safety, afraid of loneliness. And especially if we do not clearly understand who we are, what we live for, and what we may hope for, we are inclined to fight our fears through material means.

Hyperreality is what provides us with those means. Hyperreality promises us fulfillment of our desires. Watch this porn movie, and you will feel satisfied! Take out a loan, and you could be carelessly floating around in your new yacht! Buy a new tablet, it will save you so much time! Aim for the top job, then your work will finally be meaningful!

* * *

I want to put the three aforementioned basic needs at the center of the following three chapters. We could say they are three domains of life in which hyperreality promises us certainty and satisfaction. Acquire money, then you will be wealthy. Control everything, then you will be secure. Elevate your status, then you will belong.

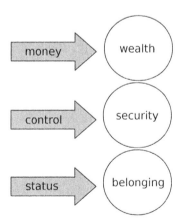

The promises of hyperreality

I: THE PROMISES OF HYPERREALITY

These promises address us individually, and this is important; but I want to discuss how they address us as a collective. The promises play a quintessential role in the shaping of our society. As a consequence, however, it becomes increasingly difficult to judge them. This might prove dangerous. It could very well be that our society unknowingly commits to a path we do not actually want to follow.

I want to take a closer look at these promises. Not to develop an all-encompassing theory of everything—which is exactly the problem of this day and age, our eagerness to reduce everything to a controllable mechanism—but rather because they help me understand how society works. I want to know whether they deliver on their promises—and if not, who is paying the price.

3

Hyperrich

*How the first promise of hyperreality,
wealth through money, is not fulfilled,
as money has its own agenda and behaves
suspiciously like a religion.*

FRIENDS OF MINE BOUGHT a very beautiful old house, right in the city centre. It was expensive, but two fulltime salaries were just enough to cover the mortgage. They worked a lot on the house to get it just right: they like perfection. You know the type: "When I buy something it has to be really good." The house is filled to the brim with nice things like an espresso machine that is more expensive than my car.

They are incredibly kind and socially aware people. We met while volunteering. It was tough for them to find the time for this. Besides both having their own jobs they also had a baby to take care of, and they often felt stressed. I asked them whether a smaller house, with less upkeep, a bit further away from the city centre, would not make them happier. But no: this house was everything they ever wanted. And they definitely both need a car of their own; not because they live that far away from their work, but because they do not want to be dependent on public transport. And what about their new home cinema set, is that really necessary? Of course! It was a very conscious purchase. After all, with two jobs and a kid, a good movie is the only way to unwind a bit at night. But—I asked carefully—would you not rather work less instead? Yes, they said, they would like to. But it's not an option: life is too expensive.

So it was no surprise that these friends soon stopped volunteering. Although they liked the work and considered it very important, they simply did not have the time. I thought of them when I read about German research showing that the average couple spends twelve minutes per day talking together. For dual earners the figure is only seven minutes. I do not know how representative this particular research was, but I do wonder whether my friends would even reach this. I also wonder whether they will ever attain what they want. Their goal is material comfort and security. They want to be in a position in which they are never short of anything. But to attain that goal they need so many possessions, all of which demand care, that I fear their desire of being carefree is actually pushing them in the opposite direction. I can still see the anxiety in their eyes when a leak in their kitchen had them struggling to get insurance money. Their insurance company was only available to consider their case during office hours, when my friends were hard at work themselves.

Hyperreality promises us wealth through money. That we will incur additional costs in pursuing it is never mentioned. I started this chapter with a personal anecdote, but I will go on now explore how this promise works on a societal level. The key notion here is *economic growth*. This growth will help us to acquire money, since it is the fundamental aim and drive of the economy. But this drive is not neutral. Money is debt, as we will find out, which is why it has such tremendous power. It drives individuals insane, but it also creates a hyperreality of financial markets, which is completely devoid of physical reality—but which drives that reality nevertheless.

Why does the economy always have to grow? I once asked the Dutch minister of economic affairs. He was—and still is—a staunch supporter of economic growth. I only work three days a week in order to be available for my neighbourhood and my family. At the time I did not earn enough to afford a car. Very environmentally friendly! But the minister could not agree with my lifestyle. "If everyone were to live like you do, I would emigrate", he said. "Macro-wise we have to grow. Growth is the key to everything."[1]

According to most mainstream economists, we simply cannot forgo growth. Without growth our wealth cannot increase, so the logic goes. The best thing I could do would be to work hard in a position for which I have been educated, so the government can spend my tax money on social workers who will play football with street youths. My kids can best be raised by child-minders, while a psychiatrist can help me to cope with the resulting stress. And in order to fight climate change, we should work more, not less, so that the collective profit can be spent on environmental scientists who can fix the problem. If we were to do it this way, the world would become a much more efficient place. This is a process we have to embrace. After all, if we do not do it, the Chinese will, and we will fall behind, which is bad.

Notice how mimetic rivalry plays a key role here. On an individual level, we continuously compare ourselves to others. When people around me want a certain coffee machine, it is very likely that I will want one for myself too. But collectively we may also become entangled in mimetic rivalry. The Chinese are copying our way of life because they desire our wealth, which forces us to grow

---

1. I have written two books about this with Freek Koster, published in Dutch only. We discovered that our society is in exactly the same situation as Keanu Reeves and Sandra Bullock in the movie *Speed*, who find themselves driving a bus loaded with a bomb. If they use the brake, they detonate the bomb, so they have to keep speeding, but after a while they discover that they will eventually run out of fuel and explode anyway. Our economic system works like this bus.

faster to maintain an advantage over the Chinese. Notice the element of anxiety again.

Of course, no one will claim that growth is their goal. Rather, growth is always said to be a means to an end. The great economist John Maynard Keynes argued the same.[2] In 1930, he had a vision. In a hundred years, he predicted, we will be four to five times as rich, and we will have to work just three hours per day to meet our needs. We will all come to the conclusion that greed is bad and contentment is good. But, he pointed out, until that time greed will be necessary. Greed makes us consume, which keeps the wheels of the economy turning, which stimulates growth and progress. As per Maslow: as long as we secure our basic necessities, development will eventually follow.

The first part of Keynes' vision became reality, tenfold. From a material standpoint, we are many times richer than we were in 1930. Besides the increased amount of calories in our dinners, we can also get twelve types of peanut butter, meat every day, more then ten screens in the house, and one or two cars per family. There are amusement parks, ambulances for animals, heart-lung machines. We have become richer, but have we also gained more time for ourselves? Seemingly, no. On average we work just as much as we used to, only now with more stress involved. In my country, 10 percent of the population has burnout symptoms, and an incredibly large part of the people need antidepressants to cope with life.

Keynes failed to notice something very important: the difference between needs and desires. Our desires are, in fact, not static but dynamic, and they grow along with the desires of others. Perhaps you happen to be that one ascetic person who is content with eating dry bread, does not need much more than one bicycle, and is perfectly fine with camping in the woods during holiday season. Still, you too will have to adapt. The dynamism is ingrained in the way the economy works. It is structural, to the extent that it is increasingly difficult to escape. It is either growth, or economic collapse.

2. See Skidelsky and Skidelsky, *How Much is Enough?*

One of human's core needs, as we found in the previous chapter, is material comfort. Or, put more generally: wealth. The goal of the economy, one might argue, is the creation of wealth, of value through the scarcity of resources. But "wealth" and "value" are more than what we can calculate. If interpreted more broadly, "profit" is much more than what can be expressed in numbers. Part of the profit of a society is material production, obviously, but another part is the satisfaction of having colleagues or making a meaningful contribution to a company.

To generate such profits, we use supplies of *capital*. We have nature, which provides us with resources we can use, and our heads, which we can fill up with tons of knowledge. We have the rule of law, ensuring trust amongst ourselves and between us and our government. We use all of these types of capital, whether they be natural, human, social, cultural, or financial, in the economic process to produce value. All forms of capital have to be carefully nurtured so we can live off the "interest" they produce, a process we recognize as the growth of wealth.

In this way growth can be seen as an end result: the outcome of a healthy economic process. The treacherous thing about this sound goal, however, is that it is increasingly understood in a much narrower sense. Finance ministers present the national budget once a year, which makes no mention of wealth in the broad sense but only of purchasing power. This is not only the fault of economists and politicians but also of journalists, bankers, and civil society groups. They want a figure on everything. That is why we use gross domestic product (GDP) to gauge wealth, expressed in euros or dollars. GDP is nothing more than the total of all formal economic transactions that take place.

This is a serious inhibition to our understanding of wealth. If we build a factory in a nature reserve, which then contaminates the water, the government will have to clean it up, while prosecutors charge those responsible. Every one of these steps boosts the GDP. The economy grows. But does anyone create wealth?

If from now on we all bought twice as much food as we actually eat, throwing away the leftovers every day, this would increase economic growth. So would an animal feed producer deforesting the Amazon to grow soybeans. In the end, all of these produce economic growth. But wealth does not increase. In fact, some forms of "capital"—food, rainforests—will have decreased, and should be subtracted from the total. But since calculating them is incredibly complex, we skip this step and go on doing everything we can to boost GDP, since our entire economic system is based on it. To gain more of it we split up firms, force countries into severe austerity, compel mothers on welfare to work, and construct roads through nature reserves.

In other words, collectively we are so inclined to fulfil our need for material comfort that we chain up ourselves ever more tightly to the mechanisms we believe will provide it. But our desires grow along with what we have. What follows is that we squander our capital and as a consequence undermine our own wealth. This leads to an observation we will make more often: hyperreality looks great on the outside, but in fact parasitizes our reality.

If we look at reality, and not the hyperreality of government budget presentations, we notice that our wealth is rapidly declining. It does not matter much which graph we pick out—the number of fish in the ocean, the area of forest on earth, the amount of metal, oil, or phosphorus in the ground, the quality of the atmosphere or farmland, the number of animal and plant species—they all show a worrying downward trend. And this is only the "natural capital". "Social capital" is harder to express in numbers, but looking at the amount of people who burn out around me, I am sure that much of it is being depleted. In poorer countries, these effects are most pressing. But according to Herman Daly, a renowned ecological economist who has developed measures of wealth in the broader sense, even in Western countries our wealth has declined since 1980, he explained to me in an interview.

However, we have witnessed *apparent* growth. We have managed to make the system grow by infusing it with large amounts of financial capital. In the 90s, we did this by taking out huge mortgages on houses. Everyone started investing, which caused the stock markets to rise. Since the system was apparently working, growing inflation was glossed over. But this is not much more than a massive pyramid scheme. Economic growth is no longer based on real value creation, but mostly on increasing expectations. We in the West create little real value. Our enormous growth in material wealth is mostly the result of cheap production in other parts of the world. We ourselves cannot even produce enough to pay off our debts.

We cannot grow indefinitely. When biologists find something that does, they call it cancer. This must inevitably lead to a crisis—but more on that later.

* * *

So how about we collectively agree to stop our craze for growth? Unfortunately, that is impossible, because of the nature of growth. It has become indispensable. Growth is expressed through money. To have built our society on economic growth essentially means we have built it on money.

I want to expand on this, because it is so important to understanding who we are. It is quite something to have the structure of our whole civilization depend on a single mechanism. Money is something we fundamentally misunderstand. Many believe that money was originally intended as a means for barter and has become more important on its own over time. This is incorrect. In most barter societies, people worked with forms of informal and locally organized credit based on complex rules and relationships. Money, however, has always been connected to military empires. The current paper money system was created in European countries by kings who wanted the support of the nobility in their wars. In exchange for their gold, the noblemen were given a debt certificate that afforded them the right to a part of the king's treasury. These debt certificates were increasingly used as an active means of payment.

Money still is a debt certificate. It is not a neutral medium of exchange. It is a contract testifying of a relationship nested in debt. These contracts are electronically created by commercial banks or governments—in the case of obligations—that hold an account with the central bank. The (electronic) debt certificates are lent to people who promise they will pay back the amount with interest, and promise to be economically active in order to do so. For this reason, money is not a possession, it is a liability. It is a symbol of one person's debt to another, and that symbol has ended up in your pocket in the shape of a paper note. But it is a social force. The money in your pocket is always on its way back—with profit—to its original owner. Money always looks for more money. *The devil always shits on the biggest heap*, as the Dutch saying goes, and it's right. Money is a force that creates riches for those who have it already. As a consequence, "developing" countries typically pay more in interest than they receive in the shape of development aid.

Money is not neutral. Since it entails a contract of debt, not everything is of interest to money. It only sees the things one can calculate—it sees "wealth" in the narrowest sense, but not what cannot be calculated. It considers material things more important than immaterial ones. As such, it also influences societal values. Money prefers discontented people to contented people, since discontent is a stimulus that keeps the machine running. In theory, no one considers money to be the most valuable thing in their lives. Yet in practice it determines our values.

Capitalism is the economic system *par excellence* that is fundamentally structured by money. And it only works as long as we trust the system. At its core, money is a matter of trust. Money is a matter of belief. The word *credit* is derived from *credo*, which means belief. Hence, capitalism is a belief system, and an economic crisis is a crisis of belief.

This is interesting, since capitalism does not have a sacred text. There is no dogma, one might say, only a cult. The German-Jewish philosopher Walter Benjamin postulated this in 1921, in his treatise *Kapitalismus als Religion* (Capitalism as Religion)[3]. According to him, capitalism is the "cult of debt". Debt is indispensable. We have to incur debts in order to keep consumption up to the mark. And because we are stuck, it is very difficult to criticize it. Much like the religions of old, there are fetishes and symbols that

3. Benjamin, *'Kapitalismus as Religion'*.

we ascribe spiritual power to. Consider the credit rating agencies' reports that can push countries to the brink of economic collapse. Or central bankers, the high priests of the cult, who can make the stock markets tumble in the blink of an eye.

* * *

So, our money-based system exhibits religious characteristics. This also explains why it is not merely a personal desire for more that makes us focus on money. It is not necessary for us to personally believe in the promise that money affords us wealth. After all, we are collectively indebted to those that provide us with money. Our collective debt casts a long shadow, forcing us to make more money. Most, if not all, countries have massive debts that run into the billions, which is why we have to cut down on healthcare, development aid or nature conservation. The creditors, the people that receive interest, are the ones that have enough money to hand out loans. In the long term the increase in wealth is mostly private, while public wealth is decreasing, as the French economist Thomas Piketty has demonstrated.

Economic growth has become an inescapable mechanism. This is one of the key points of my story: we often talk about "raising awareness", about morality, but those discussions are fruitless if at the same time we build a world in which money and other autonomous forces dictate our path.[4]

Once I talked to a few managers of Royal Dutch/Shell to ask why they had stopped their investments in wind energy and were even divesting. Had they lost money on it? No, they replied, but the profit margin was too small for the shareholders. The mighty oil company has to abide by the demands of the stock market, and is completely unfree to make independent choices. I once asked a director of the ING Bank why under her rule they invested so much in weapons producers, but the answer was exactly the same: the shareholders force us to deliver the biggest profit possible. In much the same way, countries are indebted to bondholders. If we

---

4. To see how civilized people can be co-opted by immoral bank policies, read Luyendijk, *Among the Bankers*.

do not pay off those debts, with interest of course, the financial markets will collapse. We cannot let this happen, because we are dependent on them. In fact, the system uses its weakness to manipulate us. We have to cater to its demands because otherwise it will collapse and then we're nowhere.

Journalist Thomas Friedman coined the term *electronic herd*, the mob of millions of anonymous traders spread across the planet, investing in anything from which they expect a profit.[5] When their confidence in a certain market or product dissipates, they pull out their investments, creating havoc. The credit rating agencies who give ratings to Spain, Russia or Argentina, are the "bloodhounds" of the herd, with the power to drive a country into ruin.

* * *

We can zoom in even closer on the financial markets, since developments continue. Even the herd can be optimized. Financial trade itself is increasingly automated. Nowadays, computer programs, which calculate the perfect moment to sell and buy stock, execute seventy percent of all stock market transactions worldwide.

In other words: machines are taking over the financial trade. Not only do they make the calculations, they are also becoming the decision makers. This practice, called algorithmic trading, has in recent years conquered the financial system. From the smallest investment funds to the biggest banks: computer code and algorithms are in charge. Complex programs analyse sales figures, governmental reports, and other financial data to find investment opportunities.

A large part of these transactions entails what is called the "ultrashort term". These are transactions that aim to turn a profit from the smallest of price fluctuations. This so-called "high-frequency trading" takes place in milliseconds. But even this can become faster. Some trade offices now communicate through microwaves (a type of electromagnetic radiation, not the cooking appliance) instead of fiberglass cables. Light travels faster through

5. Friedman, *Lexus and the Olive Tree.*

air than through fiberglass. The investment has cost millions, but the trade offices who jumped on this bandwagon can now get their signals from New York City to Chicago in 2.75 milliseconds. The laggards who stayed behind still need 6.75 milliseconds to do the same thing.

For the economy as a whole, this doesn't matter at all, except that the system has now become so complex that it can cause itself to crash while making it impossible for humans to determine the cause. This happened, for example, during the "flash crash" of 2011, when computers malfunctioned for twenty minutes and made 900 billion dollars of market value disappear. The stock market quickly recovered, but billions of dollars changed hands. Something similar happened during that same year to the sugar and cacao market, in which prices have become much more unpredictable. Auditors still cannot explain exactly what happened in this complex system. The machine has become the master of the stock market.

* * *

Money creates its own hyperreality. In the financial world, "representations" of reality—statistics and numbers—have started to lead a life of their own.[6] Reality itself is being forgotten. At best it is an obstacle to increasing profit. Even the representations (like shares or obligations) are cut up and resold in the shape of financial products. The sum of all financial products is ten times the actual value of all material things on earth put together. The world of finance has become a world in which people believe the boundaries of time and space have been broken down, in which they want growth to continue indefinitely, and all in good conscience, for as long as everyone rationally pursues their own interest, the market will efficiently provide balance and optimal distribution. At least, that is what the economics books argue.

In reality, there is no balance in the financial markets. The prices of shares, obligations, and other products tell us little about

---

6. The notion that the stock market is an image of reality, but is more and more perceived as reality, was explained to me by the German philosopher Joseph Vogl, author of *The Specter of Capital*.

the real value that is at its core. These values are virtual, they are established on markets where all kinds of (mimetic) sentiments, influences, computer systems, and power interests are at play. When push comes to shove, nobody knows the fundamentals under all the numbers and statistics. In hyperreality, the boundary between real and fake is no longer distinguishable.

But hyperreality does parasitize on reality. The financial market's profits have to come from somewhere—from the productive sectors of the economy—and, in the end, behind every abstract financial number is a real human being who has to pay for it. For a long time we have managed to postpone the moment when we will have to pay our dues, by growing fast enough for everyone to profit. But natural reality has its boundaries. Someday, growth will meet its end.

This was the cause of the credit crisis of 2007-2008. Growth stagnated, which resulted in people not being able to pay off their debts, a problem banks were not prepared for. In an attempt to alleviate the crisis, governments took over those debts that could only be paid for with new money; in other words, new debt certificates. Instead of accepting the limits of nature, of reality, we ignored them. You could argue the same for the coronacrisis of 2020. This virus was a real problem, part of the real world, killing real people and posing real limits to economic growth. But since our system doesn't function without growth, our governments had to invent it anyway, by creating trillions of debt. It is a trap from which ultimately there is no escape. Debt has to be paid or deflected to someone else. This is only possible through devaluation, inflation, or bankruptcy. Someday we will have to face this reality.

Thanks to all these interventions, the weight of central banks has become enormous. Evidently, they are the ones now dictating economic policy. We can hardly call this democratic anymore. All we are left to serve is financial stability. When central banks believe it necessary to sell a country's biggest port to Chinese investors, privatize the railway network and fire its employees, or to cut civil servants' pensions, it will happen. The technicians will solemnly argue that it is sad, yet necessary for the system.

* * *

This chapter began with the first promise of hyperreality: acquire money, and you will receive material comfort. Wealth through money. This can take hold of individuals, but also of entire societies, which then speak of "growth". We have seen that it is very difficult to break out of this situation due to the central role that has been given to money. Because of this role, money can impose its own values on the collective. It is inescapable, even if we acknowledge that the money system is in fact dangerous for our actual wealth. It is the classic story of the means becoming more important than the ends (more on this later).

Stand back and look, and the whole situation is very odd. We have given life to something we do not want. We agree that the economy has to change, to be more sustainable and fair, and yet we are not able to execute the change. This is a conclusion we will come back to in the coming chapters. Somehow, all of us mean well—well, most of us—but there are forces that push us in another direction. It is as if you were at a theatre performance, but you could see the performance because the entire crowd is standing up. Why are people standing up? Because everyone else is. Now it is impossible to get people to sit down again.

Perhaps the people in the front row have the most responsibility, but the mistake flows directly from our own desires and the accompanying fear of want. All of us desire material comfort, but because money promises us the means to reach that goal, slowly but steadily we start to desire money itself. If eventually the additional hidden costs are brought out in the open, as well as the power structures behind the financial system, we can no longer get rid of them. Will we still have a job next year, will our government have the money to take care of the elderly, will we ever get a pension? All this is dependent on the caprice of the financial markets. Our initial goal was material comfort and security—the very thing that is now slipping out of reach.

4

Hypersecure

How the second promise of hyperreality, security by control, is delivering in the short term but at the cost of expensive security systems that could turn against us.

THE WORLD IS SCARY. Risks are lurking everywhere. This is disturbing for our experience of the smooth and frictionless hyperreality. Paradoxically, the risks in our well-organized world are bigger than ever. One terrorist slipping through at the airport gates can make skyscrapers collapse. One mistake in a railway computer system can cause two trains to collide. One insecure connection in a state computer can enable Iranian spies to download complete address books. One virus in a small corner of the world can kill millions. All these examples have already happened: tragedies that could have been prevented if we had controlled and checked and overseen everything better.

Control is the road to security: at least, that's what hyperreality promises us. Hyperreality is nourished on our anxieties.

But the resulting control, grip, or domination—whatever we call it—can quickly become its own justification. The security we seek can easily lead to tyranny, and we can end up saddled with control systems that have become unmanageable and monstrous.

* * *

My own country is good at controlling. We like registering and monitoring our lives. A funny but telling example is the so-called "child-following system" that my children's school has opted for. One day we had a progress meeting with my six-year old son's kindergarten teacher. We expected a nice chat about how she thought things were going, if my son was happy and when they'd organize the trip to the zoo. Instead, she came up with an elaborate graph consisting of fifteen grades, updated every three weeks, for fifteen so-called "competences", like cooperation and self-worth, for which he scored a 5.8, which was 0.9 lower than the national average, but still 0.2 better than the last time. I asked the teacher if she liked this system. She said she spent half her time categorizing six-year-olds instead of teaching them and she was fed up with all this digital stuff. What was called a child-following system looked more like a teacher-following system in the end.

This way of thinking comes along with digitalization, but it is also part of our cultural DNA. We Dutch have a historical inclination to rule by knowledge. We want to know, to measure and to register, because then we feel safe and secure. It's no accident that a century ago my country was one of the first to develop a civil registration system and a passport, in an efficient and hard-to-forge way.

The question that the designers of that system asked themselves was: how can you care for your citizens effectively, if you don't clearly know who they are? A diligent civil servant named Jacobus Lentz came up with a bright solution. He asked every municipality to create a card system with one entry for each citizen, including information on their relations and church membership. It was ingenious. For his zeal and his sharp eye for innovation he was honored by the queen herself with the communist-sounding title "civil servant of the year". "Registering is serving", was his equally communist-sounding slogan. Lentz also proposed the introduction of an obligatory national identity card, but that idea was dismissed. It was deemed inappropriate, since it would potentially regard everyone as a potential criminal.

* * *

Lentz's card system is child's play compared to the unlimited possibilities in today's era of data. With the help of digital technology we can map and archive and categorize everything we want, everything on earth and in heaven, from the most distant mountain trails to the highest stars, from pictures of our breakfast to all the music that has ever been made. Everything is searchable and analyzable; the world is at our feet.

The amount of time that we spend in this digital archive is growing and growing. This hyperreality is the space where we plan our trips, work, read news, shop, have fun and even find one-night stands. Artificial intelligence opens a whole new range of options for controlling and optimizing these areas of our lives, from Amazon's advice on what to read, to the suggestions of digital assistants like Cortana or Siri on what to do today, right through to "smart" dating sites suggesting the man or woman that best matches your profile.

A growing number of devices out in the real world are connected to the internet. This is called the internet of things. It's just a matter of time before we have smart cars that are permanently connected to road authorities, GPS services, social media and other vehicles through a load of sensors that do all the work for us. Meanwhile, the smart lamps, smart alarms, smart ovens, smart heaters, smart floors and smart streetlights are taking over the world. All are manageable though smart applications on smart phones, connected to countless servers in distant places which share their data instantaneously: all of it, as the screen assures me, in the service of achieving more safety and a better user experience.

This enables behavioral control like never before. Behavioral control means to change people's behavior step by step. Sometimes with our consent, like the running app with a trustworthy female voice telling me when to run and when to walk, or the medical app that helps me quit smoking, but sometimes without our consent. We can be "nudged" towards good and safe behavior, marketeers know. When cars communicate with each other, accidents will be prevented, even when we fall asleep behind the steering wheel. For techno-optimists this is not fundamentally different from the billboard campaigns urging us to drive safely. What's the difference between a government billboard and a personal nudge from your car assistant?

It's hard to stand against these measures. Who can be against more safety? But we are following a path that doesn't end there, and that changes the way we interact with the world around us. Technology critic Evgeny Morozov calls this tendency to try to fix all frictions with a mouse click *solutionism*: the idea that the whole world should be as efficient and frictionless as an iPhone. But the big question we should ask ourselves is: who is the designer? Who sets the norms and the standards and who draws the conclusions? It is not unimaginable that we will see the rise of a technology that prevents us from stealing, fare dodging or breaking a law. Who will set the rules and who will own the data? And what will be the effect on our politics and our morality if we are technologically prevented from making mistakes? America would have been quite different, writes Morozov, if Rosa Parks had been traveling on a smart bus that had prevented her breaking the law.[1]

Some car insurance companies charge lower rates for those who share data about their location and driving style, which is the effective equivalent of exacting a fine on those who don't want to do this. Health insurance companies urge their customers to measure their heartbeat, blood sugar and other biodata in real time. Why not charge extra for people who consume too many calories, get out of bed too late, don't exercise regularly or give birth to babies with Down's Syndrome? Those are all perceived as risks to our current way of life.

1. Morozov, *To Save Everything, Click Here.*

I: THE PROMISES OF HYPERREALITY

Let's not forget that in the end all of these commercial players have one goal: profit. Megafirms like Google, Facebook, Microsoft, Netflix or Amazon, and many other more obscure data companies, analyze and use everything we say, watch, read, write or film. By analyzing our online or offline behavior, these firms are able to provide us with a better service, and to nudge us in the direction of better and safer behavior, sometimes, or worse and more unsafe behavior at other times, but ultimately all in the service of making us buy more. We hope that artificial intelligence will give us more and more control over the world, but we could just as well ask ourselves whether we will lose control instead. I only have to think about the majority of my friends who have lost the ability to read a map and to discern east from west since they outsourced their sense of direction to Google or other driving apps.[2]

But what if it works, and if we are never lost anymore: isn't that worth it? Good question. But security and comfort come with a price tag. One of the costs is our privacy. Note that this is a misleading word if we narrow it to the issue of whether we have "something to hide" from the outside world. If I'm honest I don't really care if somebody knows something about me. The real issue is if it is acceptable that there are people who know everything about everyone—and not only know, but use this knowledge to influence us or nudge us in the direction they want us to go, without us even being aware of it.

Facebook knows that it is able to influence the emotions of its users. In a famous experiment they fed people's timelines with only optimistic or pessimistic posts without their knowing, and were able to measure that people felt more positive or negative throughout the day. The company Cambridge Analytica went a few steps further. They acquired the Facebook data of about 87 million Facebook users, through different methods and apps, both legal and illegal, and used it to build profiles of 200 million American

2. On the effect of internet on our learning capacity, see Spitzer, *Digitale Demenz* (Digital Dementia). The book is in German, but English articles and lectures are available online. Also thought-provoking is Carr, *Shallows* and *Glass Cage*.

44

citizens and many millions of people in the rest of the world. They were hired not only by Donald Trump during his first presidential campaign but also by the British Leave EU campaign and by politicians in Kenya and Brazil, among others. They were able to tell the campaigners who were swing voters and who could be influenced by which message, either factual or mendacious, and they seem to have had a tremendous effect on the outcomes.[3]

* * *

Understandably, Justice ministers are drooling at the thought of the power these digital companies are amassing. The distinction between state and market is not as strict as we sometimes think. States are doing everything they can to acquire knowledge about as many people as possible in order to try to make the world transparent and secure. The companies in their turn would be helpless without the laws, the funding and the commercial orders coming from governments. At least in the security industry, the dichotomy between state and market is fictitious.

A few years ago I visited the headquarters of Morpho, a French security company that was part of a French military conglomerate. I wanted to talk with the founder and then director of R&D, Bernard Didier. This man stood in the tradition of Jacob Lentz, the Dutch civil servant of the year. In the eighties Didier was the inventor of the current fingerprint-based passports, and he personally developed the code necessary to identify them automatically, in a time when a computer wasn't able even to get an image on a screen. He was not held back by the government because of ethical concerns, as Lentz had been. On the contrary, he was funded by the FBI to build an identification system. It was the first step towards biometric databases and systems, which he sold to more than one hundred countries, like India, for which he helped to set up a citizen registration system based on iris scans, the biggest biometrics project ever. It also helps enforcement authorities like the FBI to recognize people based on their fingerprints.

3. How internet can actually strengthen dictatorial regimes, read Morozov, *Net Delusion*.

I: THE PROMISES OF HYPERREALITY

When I visited him in Paris, Didier led me around in his showroom where I could experience the ease of the different recognition systems. I got a fake biometric passport with my picture and had to cross a fake border, without standing still. The computer recognized me without problems. *Face on the Fly,* they called this program. "This is an example about what it means to let technology serve man," Didier said, "instead of the other way around. The interest of the state is security, but the citizen wants convenience and speed."

In another corner I had to wave my hands through the kind of hand dryer you see in fancy restaurants, but this hand dryer immediately recognized my fingerprints, without direct contact. "This is our *Finger on the Fly,*" he said. "You don't dare to think about the lines that will develop at John F. Kennedy when a dangerous disease breaks out and nobody wants to be fingerprinted. This is much more hygienic."

Alongside his aim of being a market leader in biometrics, which he has achieved, Didier was very idealistic in his goals. "As long as our identity can be stolen, our possessions are not safe," he said. "Preventing this is the most important job of a state. That is my big goal. It's a question of time, maybe it will take some years, but I know that it is possible to prevent this forever."

* * *

On Wikipedia you will search in vain for Didier, but he and and his colleagues have been crucial in the way governments secure their borders. The US authorities still cooperate with Morpho, now called IDEMIA, which on its website promises innovative biometric terminals that guarantee "approved" individuals frictionless access to secured areas. The borders are not a gate anymore, guarded by big-mustached military types who slowly sweep through the stamps in your passports to see if they can find something against you. Today's border is increasingly a computer program profiling all citizens, and sorting the wanted from the unwanted.

All states are rapidly expanding their databases with the facial scans, the fingerprints, the iris scans and the destinations of all visitors. Migrants and tourists alike are added to this system when they enter, and they can be recognized whenever and wherever they are checked by enforcement authorities. One day soon, this system should able to check them out automatically if and when they walk out again.

In order not to worry their citizens, most states, including the United States and the European Union, start by collecting the data of foreigners, but the system slowly moves towards the registration of everyone. The European Union is very secretive about its ideas, since privacy is a sensitive issue, but when I called the head of the American biometrics program, who set up the whole biometric recognition system for the Department of Homeland Defense, he was very happy to explain how well the system worked against terrorists and criminals entering the country, and he boasted about the tens of thousands of records he had shared with the FBI or the local police or even friendly nations in order to catch the bad guys.

He and his European colleagues emphasize the privacy values that they adhere to when it comes to their own citizens, but it's no secret that they share this data with each other. So Europe is free to profile Americans and America is free to profile Europeans and they are allowed to peek into each other's databases.

I've been to different meetings and conferences about this topic and I have asked a lot of people exactly what problem is solved by biometric registration, but in the end I haven't met anyone who can tell me. Nobody knows exactly the seriousness of the problem of people who enter the country regularly but stay too long. Many illegal immigrants don't pass a border post. It looks like the systems create their own policy. The existing immigration systems don't function well, and that's why the industry comes up with new technology, consisting of smart borders and large scale data systems. These systems are the solution, that's the starting point: you will only truly see and what the problems are when you buy them. And policy makers and politicians? They want to show that they do everything they can to stop immigrants, so they spend millions on these toys.

When I talked to the head of the American biometrics program I asked him what would be his end goal. Would he favor a database containing all the biometric data of all the people in the world? His reply: "If it is possible to do this securely—and we have proven here that it is—and society accepts it, then my answer is yes."

We are quickly moving towards what experts call a security society. The border will be an intangible, omnipresent machine that is constantly dividing people into two categories: wanted and unwanted. This will be a permanent sorting machine, with no clear distinction between immigration policy, law enforcement and defense policy. And next to this, biometrics is on the brink of breaking through in other domains, including medical files, payment systems and telecommunications.

In the office of Morpho I was told that it is still possible to fool the system, unfortunately, by wearing fake fingerprints or lenses. So you know what's really secure? DNA. In twenty years or so there will be a database which includes the DNA of everyone. This will be foolproof.

When I walked out of the office of Morpho I opened the fake passport that I had been given in the demonstration room. Below my name they had printed a fictitious place of birth: Utopia.

* * *

A security state doesn't have to be a dictatorship where we will be tortured if we have the wrong opinions. It can be, and doubtless will be, more like a benevolent, soft monster that only wants the best for us. The sorting machine wants to protect us from people who pose a danger to our way of life. In the hyperreal world of the people who are lucky enough to be a 1 instead of a 0, there will be no sign of undocumented migrants, armed border police or even borders. That would be very upsetting. We will travel to open airports that give us a smooth and frictionless experience, and at the former border posts we will find fashion and food.

For the 0's among us life will be next to impossible. I think about a friend, Farid, who lived with us for a while. He was an undocumented migrant from Afghanistan with an extra o next to his name, because in the past he has worked for an Afghan government entangled in a civil war. The computer automatically gave him the status of *war criminal*, although he has never done anything but bookkeeping. He is a Christian, so it's very dangerous for him in Afghanistan, and he has been together with a Dutch wife for years. But the system keeps saying he is a war criminal, and he will never get documents here. This often makes his life almost unbearable; so much so that he decided to leave his wife and tries his luck in again another country where the authorities don't have his fingerprints—yet.

There is a trend towards a division between Red Zones and Green Zones, like the US created in Iraq. In the global Green Zone life will be safe and free. On the local scale there will also be Red and Green Zones. Complete residential areas are built where private security keeps the outsiders out, like the shopping malls in Brazil where the people from the favelas are not allowed to enter, or the neighborhoods in Asia where inhabitants can only enter by showing their fingerprints. In the Red Zones there is only security for people who can afford it. This is a dangerous time bomb for everyone, that's why control will be scaled up. In the Red Zones this will be enforced by planes and drones. In the Green Zones, control will be noiseless.

* * *

China gives us a glimpse of this secure future. An example was visible to the world during the outbreak of the coronavirus at the beginning of 2020. Within weeks the Chinese government introduced a new app to track the health status of all citizens in certain areas. People signed up through wallet apps they already know, and were assigned a QR code with a color. Green meant no risk, and a yellow or red code was given to people who had had contact with an infected person. Yellow and red people were denied entrance to many locations and roads. The information behind the code was based on data on plane, train and bus bookings, but also on location data. A green code could turn inexplicably into a yellow code after being close to another yellow or red code. Secretly, location data was shared with the police. The question is again: who decides? Many people shared their anger online after their code changed to another color without any justification. Nobody seemed to be able to explain how the system decided what made someone green, yellow or red. Yet Western countries were jealously watching the Chinese efficiency, ready to copy their measures if necessary.

Data is not the same as wisdom, however. The Chinese government was quick to praise itself for its effective containment of the coronavirus, but in reality the situation got out of hand because the the doctor who discovered the virus, Li Wenliang, was immediately silenced by the authorities. When he warned colleagues about the new disease, he was summoned to the Public Security Bureau where he had to sign a letter accusing him of making false comments that had "severely disturbed the social order". When he got back to work, he contracted the disease and died. For omniscient dictators, control is more important than truth. Yet without truth, it is hard to keep control.

Still, dictators have power to decide for millions of people what is true and what is false. The Chinese communist party even regards certain ideas or groups as dangerous viruses, be it Uyghurs speaking their own language and wearing headscarves, or Christians meeting in house churches stating that no man is omniscient, or doctors warning that hospitals make mistakes. Different Chinese cities and authorities are rolling out facial recognition, tracking methods and social credit systems, all for the higher goal of exterminating bad thoughts and increasing security. We won't need red or green zones if we have red or green people.

Apparently, most citizens, also many Westerners, are willing to accept the power of the state, in exchange for the higher goal of security. A pervasive police state might be scary, but not as scary as terrorists and viruses. People tend to think they have nothing to hide. But what the complacent citizens seem to forget is that they are not in charge of deciding what is worthy of hiding. They also forget that definitions of what should be hidden, what is dangerous, and who is the enemy tend to change over time. We in the West don't seem to be much different, given the vast amounts of data we are willing to share either with authorities or with commercial parties, all for the higher goal of reducing the risks to our rich and convenient way of life.

* * *

There's a sting in the tail of Lentz's story, though. Just after his idea for the passport was dismissed, there was a change of government. The new government did not have ethical objections to regarding all citizens as potential criminals. Lentz was allowed to create new identity papers that were impossible to counterfeit. They contained a signature, picture and fingerprint, made possible with the most advanced punch-card technology, printed on special paper with a watermark of the Dutch lion and a text that only became visible when held before a lamp. Lentz placed a copy of all these papers in a central databank called the Cartotheek, in The Hague, the city of international law. Seven million citizens in a card box.

And effective it was. When the new government, in 1941, decided to detain all the country's Jews, they were very happy to use the Carthotheek. Lentz had marked all the Jewish identity cards with a large J and a black clip, so it was easy for loyal civil servants to pick the right ones out. The consequence was disastrous for the Jewish population. 85 percent of them died, 105.000 people, a higher percentage than in Germany. This of course had never been Lentz's purpose, but he did not blame himself either. After the Second World War he was sentenced to jail for three years. According to the judges he was no Nazi but had collaborated with them out of "wrong love for population registers".[4]

That tragedy was the result of the evil choices of others. But if we acknowledge that humanity has a tendency to make evil political choices now and then, we would perhaps be better off if we didn't give her too much power. Unfortunately, this power is growing fast, and seemingly with its own will. Just like money, control

---

4. A lot has been written in Dutch on the interaction between the Dutch bureaucracy and the Nazis, see also Hannah Arendt, *Eichmann in Jerusalem*.

is a strong power that self-replicates. Control only leads to more control. Just as in the case of money, we may be friendly, good citizens, but that doesn't mean we are not still cogs in the control machine.

* * *

The message of this chapter is that an obsession with security can ultimately lead to violence. I focused on the example of the security state, but another very serious example is the nuclear arms race. The quest for more security actually puts our world in peril, as is shown for example by Eric Schlosser in his thrilling account of near-accidents with nuclear weapons[5].

Even more terrifying is what Daniel Ellsberg told me after the publication of his memoirs *The doomsday machine in* 2017. Ellsberg became famous as a whistle blower during the Vietnam War, but years before he had already discovered top secret information about nuclear planning. As a defense specialist in the sixties he found out that the Pentagon, in case of a Soviet attack, was willing to kill 600 millions of people. The planners intended to annihilate China along with Russia, not because the two countries were allies but because the planners didn't have the logistical capacity to run two separate models.

Technology has become much more sophisticated, and so has the Pentagon, but still the final stage in the escalation ladder is a war which would kill Russians, Chinese and Americans alike, and "every living being on earth bigger than a squirrel", because of the nuclear winter which will inevitably follow a large-scale nuclear war, as Ellsberg said. Ultimately, our nuclear "defense" policy is based on a threat of collective suicide.[6]

In the end, security—the second promise of hyperreality—will prove false. Security is a necessity for us all. But because we don't limit our desire for total control, we create powers that we can't control at all.

5. Schlosser, *Command and Control*.
6. Ellsberg, *The Doomsday Machine*.

5

Hyperconnected

How the third promise of hyperreality—belonging through status—has hidden costs and leads to a mass society that makes real belonging more difficult.

THE PREVIOUS TWO CHAPTERS discussed structural developments that might feel a bit distant or complex to fully keep us interested. It often doesn't keep us awake at night. What does keep us awake, though, are the people around me. What to do about our relationships, our child's behaviour, the opinion of a colleague about us: these bother us much more than abstract problems like the economy or the security state. That's why we have to focus on the impact of hyperreality to our relationships, the most important thing we have in our lives.

In this chapter, we will see that hyperreality encourages us to be successful and cool as a means of "belonging." This chapter will first delve into how this promise takes effect on the societal level. To do so, again we draw on René Girard. In contrast to the previous chapters about money and control, we will not find a "system" here that threatens us. Yet we can see a few developments one might at least call mechanisms, which are difficult to challenge. We will look at two examples: the competitive economy and (social) media, since both cause us to increasingly behave like anonymous participants in a mass society.

* * *

Think about the endless liquor advertisements, whose marketeers studied human nature well: parties with loud beats and toned butts, handsome men and sexy women, neon lit and engulfed by an air of temptation, the dancing bodies rubbing up against each other play into our hidden orgiastic fantasies. Then, the music suddenly stops—what happened? The liquor, the liquor! There he is, the mixologist, with a slick haircut and broad shoulders. A wave of euphoria cascades over the dance floor, and the mixologist and the liquor are praised in ecstatic chorus. Even the music seems to listen to him, and everyone is laughing, and everyone is one sexy, vibrating unity of nothing but euphoric people.

These marketeers are appealing to lust. But what kind of lust? To me, it seems to go beyond erotic lust. Behind that type of lust there is also a lust for community: a community of hip, cool, accomplished, sexy people of which you can be a part. By doing so, these companies communicate one of the strongest promises of hyperreality: be cool and you can be one of us.

In a lecture to students in 1944, the English writer C.S. Lewis explained that there is a stronger desire in Man than greed or lust.

> I believe that in all men's lives at certain periods, and in many men's lives at all periods between infancy and extreme old age, one of the most dominant elements is the desire to be inside the local 'Ring' and the terror of being left outside.[1]

With the "Ring" Lewis means the inner circle, the Society, the people in the know.

1. Lewis, *Inner Ring*, §9.

This desire is one of the great permanent mainsprings of human action. It is one of the factors which go to make up the world as we know it—this whole pell-mell of struggle, competition, confusion, graft, disappointment, and advertisement, and if it is one of the permanent mainsprings then you may be quite sure of this. Unless you take measures to prevent it, this desire is going to be one of the chief motives of your life, from the first day on which you enter your profession until the day when you are too old to care.[2]

The great economic and technological systems we have discussed are fuelled by the first two basic desires of humans: get rich and rule the world. But there is another desire which might be even stronger: belonging, not being left out. It is a desire born out of our need for community and relationships, and our fear of ending up alone. Hyperreality promises us fulfilment of that desire and a mitigation of that fear. It promises us status and recognition. Coolness. Yet much as is the case with money and power, hyperreality doesn't show us the hidden additional costs that come with accepting its promises. The way of coolness is blind to everything uncool.

Marketers know how it works. In one of their liquor commercials, we see visitors getting a stamp on their hand. The party that we want to go to is a private party. The party we like to be seen at is a party where only the inner circle is invited, and some people are left out by definition. And that little aspect of reality is what hyperreality forgets to mention.

* * *

It is astounding how well the word *cool* has stood the test of time amongst all kinds of hip words (like the word *hip*) that come into fashion from time to time and fade out again soon afterward. Cool does not fizzle out. Cool stays cool. Cool remains independent, untouchable, and self-assured. Cool like ice, like the night, cool like the rock star who will not take off his shades, not even for the

2. Lewis, *Inner Ring*, §16.

Pope. Cool still breathes the coolness of the slaves in the United States who originally used the word to indicate their wise, patient, and generous attitude, which saved them some face in relation to the plantation owners by whom they were used.

Through music the word spread across the globe. But more than any other word it has become a product of marketeers. The ideal image of Western culture has long been the Marlboro man, the confident unshaven pioneer who gets off his horse as the sun sets, to light his cigarette, all in a cool manner of course. His work is done, tamed some buffalos, got the girl, and no one can touch him. He is his own master. Nowadays he is not allowed to smoke anymore, he might even practice yoga, but his attitude is still cool.

Be yourself, the culture of cool tells us. But can we do that? When I go to a party I want to look unique, but in reality I am finetuning my style to the group: the aim is to be just "unique" enough to get recognition, but not too much to cross the unspoken but clearly defined borders. Like everyone else, I cannot do without admiration. Even the Marlboro man who is "being himself" would be miserable without the camera affording him attention, and probably would not make the other side of the prairie without antidepressants if not for that attention.

Girard's mimetic notion makes it clear: we do not desire the sunsets, the perfect look, a horse, or even a partner; we desire the desire of the other, We desire recognition. We want those things because someone else wants them; someone we look up to as a role model. For some things, that is no problem. Everyone can look at the sunset or walk around the prairie unshaven. But it gets more tricky when it is about a horse, or a man or a woman. We want them for ourselves. If there is another candidate, this desire grows even stronger, and this probably goes for the other as well. In other words: we become jealous rivals, simultaneously the role model as well as the admirer of the other. We want what our role model desires, but most of all we want his desire.

Designers and marketers know this. Commercials are barely about things, but about the role models who have those things. If George Clooney drinks coffee with such swagger, if such sexy people show up at these private parties—then a self-respecting global citizen cannot stay behind. We often think we can explain this from the perspective of erotic desire. Indeed, do not all men want to be like Clooney because they know women will swoon over their perfect jawline? No, the mimetic theory tells us, it is the other way around: they want those women mostly because Clooney wants them—and all other men around him watching what is happening. If our erotic desires really were so independent, there would only be fat women on TV like on Renaissance paintings. Human beings desire what their role models desire, and this drives fashion forward. Fashion is the method *par excellence* by which we position ourselves in the hierarchy of rivalry.

* * *

Cool is a mimetic concept. On a deserted island somewhere in the ocean, you cannot be cool. Cool is the product of copycat behaviour. This on its own is not necessarily a bad thing. Copycat behaviour helps children to learn and develop skills. In this way, imitation is a positive process, because the role model (a parent) cannot become a rival. The distance is too great. But Girard warns us: when we get closer to our role model and start to look like it more and more, that role model can itself become an obstacle for us (and vice versa) which will push us into a vicious cycle of competition. Love and hate are dangerously close to each other.

According to Girard, mimetic desire is the origin of violence—between groups, but also within them. Throughout history, humanity has found a way to channel such rivalry: by projecting it onto a third party. This is the scapegoat mechanism, a second important concept for which Girard is well-known. By blaming and destroying another individual, or even an entire group, people will believe they are ridding themselves of evil, which creates unity amongst themselves.

Recently I experienced this mechanism first-hand. I was relaxing by a small lake, close to my home. Good-looking men and women were intermingling, acting as cool as possible, while wearing minimal clothing. Not to do some actual swimming of course:

most people were there to check each other out from behind their sunglasses. The mimetic desire was so intense, you could almost taste it.

At some point there was an altercation. A couple of girls were shouting "pervert" at a middle-aged man. "Get lost!" they were shouting. Why? "He was jerking off!" The man took his bicycle immediately and left in a matter of seconds. So far all this was not too interesting. It is not unlikely that this unshaven man did in fact justify the accusations. The most remarkable thing, though, was that all of a sudden everyone started talking to each other. Bystanders came to the aid of the girls and shouted at the the man to "Get out of here!" Relieved, we laughed at the incident. And the odd thing was: I felt that relief too. All of a sudden I was part of the group. *We get each other,* I thought; *this is where the cool people are.* We're not like that pervert! Suddenly, good vibes were all around.

Then I thought: belonging to the inner circle is apparently just as much one of my fundamental desires as anyone else's. And I too use the outsider as a stepping stone to get there.

Here too we have to recognize that behind all of our desires is a natural need. An acquaintance of mine once visited a children's home in Romania. She was shocked at the sight of the babies there. They lay there in a vegetative state, apathetic, without crying, because the attendants did not have the time to give them individual care or caress them. The children's home deliberately did not hire additional volunteers to be able to do so. They tried it once, but once the babies got some attention they livened up. They became attached to others, they became people who laughed and talked. But once the volunteers left they would start crying. For the children's home staff it was unmanageable to take care of tens of crying babies, so they continued without the help of volunteers.

Without relationships, we are no one. Without relationships we do not develop into individuals with our own identity. Humans are relational creatures. Without others, we would not have a personality. We are made to belong and we cannot go without acknowledgement of our being. A good society enables all to fulfill this desire.

Our society puts a lot of emphasis on economic relationships in achieving that fulfillment. This is not a ridiculous idea, since there are few things as satisfying as doing meaningful work together. The problem is that our economy, the process that should provide us with those jobs, is being fueled by competition and rivalry. Hence, it cannot satisfy everyone at once. Achievement and status are relative. Achievement for one person necessarily means loss for another. And yet it remains the motor of the private sector, and increasingly of the public sector. Even professors, energy suppliers, and dentists have to compete with each other, because then they will start to work more efficiently, which should be beneficial to the overall economy. After all, we need that, in order to stay ahead of the Chinese. Thus, education has to be "performance orientated". We have to perform even better than before! And we have to stimulate boys and girls to get STEM degrees to make our knowledge economy the best in the world.

Our economy is becoming more efficient and more flexible, which offers great opportunities to the achievers. But it also creates losers. People who are less intellectual, digital, or flexible are excluded. Obviously there have always been big differences throughout history. There were nobles and serfs, princes and tramps. What is new, however, is that society is permeated by the idea that one's life is makeable. Everyone can fit in and belong, as long as you try hard enough. You can be cool. You have to be cool. According to sociologists this is a recipe for resentment. Not everyone will be deemed societally successful. So this really is a new phenomenon, historically. There have been times with much more injustice than today, but humans did not know any better. According to Girard this has changed due to the introduction of Judaeo-Christian thought. This enabled people to see injustice as evil, and to want to stand up for the victims of said injustice. God is on the side of the oppressed, not the oppressors.

Girard found this liberating. But this may also lead to what filled Nietzsche with disgust about the weakness of so-called

Christians: a cult of victimhood, an enormous resentment among people who know they have rights but fail to climb the stairs. I can see this in the neighbourhood where I live, which is quite poor; not poor as in being hungry, but in the sense that they feel excluded and worthless. There is a lot of resentment visible in their faces. Many people here are kind and generous, but many others live as victims. Some sit at home, lost, watching TV or waiting for social security. Others opt for radical Islam promising victory over all bad guys or vote for nationalistic politicians promising to stop the "tsunami of job-stealing immigrants".

The same happens internationally. An increasingly smaller group of people (to which we belong) possesses a growing share of wealth. Many people are redundant to the world economy, but the difference with previous times is that they witness on TV the lives of the rich, and they want it too. Combined with certain ideologies this may lead to a sense of victimhood that has the potential of completely disrupting society.

And so we witness a variety of ways in which status leads to exclusion, whether it be through mimetic group processes or through the laws of the gig economy. The world is becoming smaller and people are coming closer together, but the social distance between them is ever growing.

* * *

In a world in which young people learn early on that it is up to them to make the most of life, they are hit all the harder when they do not succeed. And most of the time, a lot more does not work out than does. In fact, while the number of achievements in our life remains more or less the same, those feats that we cannot accomplish are ever growing in number. Our phones and the internet have brought us in contact with numerous other people to compare ourselves with. Or rather, with the hyperreal personality that they constructed as an improved version of their self.

I see more and more clever insights that I could not make. I come across more interesting articles which I simply do not have the time to engage with. I see more photos of places I will never visit. I see more cool things than I will ever be able to make part of my own life. Even if you—very creatively—came up with the idea of making envelopes of used wallpaper, just as an example, you will find that it has already been done on Pinterest; with half a million likes of course.

The grass is always greener on the other side. But now you can see the best grass anywhere, already owned by someone else. I still refuse to own a smartphone, but my family are all enthusiastic participants in the family WhatsApp group. Family news, witty remarks and baby movies are all shared fanatically. It is nice, to stay in touch this way. We have grown so used to it, in only a few years, that we can barely realize how revolutionary this new aspect of life is, and the immense effect it has on us. But I still remember one of the first times this happened to me. My parents were on a trip to Spain, just to take a break in the offseason. While cold rain was tapping the windows at home, my sister-in-law showed me a photo my mother had just sent to all the family members, from her sun-soaked balcony in Malaga. I immediately caught myself feeling something: jealousy. I hated being stuck working in the rainy Netherlands while she was drinking piña coladas in the sun. Watching holiday pictures after their return, together, on a couch, that was something I liked to do. But to be confronted with it this directly, and so close too . . . Why was I not there? This taught me that closeness is not necessarily always a good thing in relationships. In healthy relationships, closeness and distance should be balanced.

Thomas Hobbes talked about a similar sensation in the seventeenth century. He did not care much, he wrote, if he as a pedestrian was passed by a carriage pulled by eight horses. But if he was riding a carriage with two horses, and one with four horses passed by him, that was much worse. The more people become alike, the more resentment is likely to take hold.

Many consider social media as simply a medium of communication. But every medium brings its own content. As Marshall McLuhan famously said: "The medium is the message." Every communication medium has its own reductionism. Social media display relationships through a filter of status. This is not my personal judgement; it is exactly how Zuckerberg and his Harvard buddies designed Facebook: to rank girls. It was made to be a coolness index, to show how culturally interesting you are, and all the friends you have. Liking and being liked, that is what it is all about. Not only does this lead to an endless process of comparison, but also to a culture in which people are increasingly preoccupied with marketing themselves and perceiving of themselves as a piece of social capital they have to develop. If we are to be honest, there is no denying that the fear of being excluded, of not being seen, is central.

This goes for other social media as well. They have become marketplaces of attention, in which value is measured by your ability to stand out in the crowd. A massive gap has developed between people with social skills and contacts—those people on which the gig economy is focused—and the people who do not have access to these things. As is the case with any market, there is a markedly commercial component. Twitter, Amazon, Google, Facebook and their Asian counterparts have more knowledge about our social connections than any organization in history has ever had. This can be monetized. Besides your friend list, your emails, updates, likes, and photos are all used to generate income from advertisements. Even if you do not have an account and are just visiting an online page which happens to have a like button, your online behavior is being recorded. This directly touches on the mechanisms of money and control from the previous chapters and influences the dimensions of the traditional economy. Here again, hyperreality looks like a virtual world, which is without boundaries and which contains endless possibilities—but everything that happens within it has consequences for the material world.

* * *

I want to reiterate that these consequences are not always negative. All media bring with them risks as well as opportunities. New media may help in maintaining long-distance friendships. They enable us to discover music from around the globe, to rally people behind a common cause, to circumvent authoritarian censorship, to work together efficiently.

But what may offer opportunities to one, may diminish them for someone else. The German psychiatrist Manfred Spitzer reviews all research on digital media in his book *Digital Dementia*[3]. Some of this research has found that adult Facebook users with many Facebook friends tend to have a lot of friends offline as well. Facebook seems to uphold the network of many of its users.

Research from the Californian Stanford University, however, finds the opposite to be the case amongst young girls, Spitzers says. Their research was conducted among 3461 eight to twelve year old readers of the magazine *Discovery Girl*. This research is a couple of years old, but already back then the time spent by these girls on social media amounted to an average of 6.9 hours per day. In comparison, they spent about two hours per day interacting face to face with friends. As it turns out, girls who spend more time online have fewer friends offline. They tend to feel more like an outsider, sleep less, and have a more negative outlook overall. Only ten percent of the girls finds that online friendships are generative of positive feelings.

Those who learned—before there were social media—to enter into real relationships, can benefit from social media. Those who have not acquired those skills yet, like younger people, may actually become isolated by it. My 12-year old son, who has a very social character, told me he hardly talks to his friends at school. Everybody is staring down to their screens all the time between classes. This is no exaggeration. Not a minute passes without their screens.

This is detrimental to regions of the human brain that are responsible for empathy, and as a consequence relationships develop less well. After all, regions of the human brain grow when they are being used, according to the brain specialist Spitzer. But our brain needs to pay very thorough attention to gauge the psychological and moral dimensions of a situation. The more we are distracted, the more superficial our interactions are, which makes it all the

3. Spitzer, *Digitale Demenz.*

more difficult to be truly involved with someone else's life. Brains that are not given the opportunity to exercise in interacting with others will become less developed, and hence will not become what they could have been in adult form. Spitzer's conclusion: digital media undermine our abilities to grow up as social beings.

Social media show clearly how intense the interaction can become between the human desire for status and a system that monetizes the satisfaction of that desire. And, again, how this system is incredibly difficult to turn around, creates its own dynamic, and demands participation from everyone.

In a world increasingly without titles, ranks, and classes, but with more and more contacts, friends, and "likes", we can compare ourselves with a growing number of others. While it becomes harder to have durable relationships, the differences between others and ourselves are shrinking. The processes of mimesis and rivalry, which have always existed, have been globalized. Just think of the rapidly changing hit songs and fashion that travel across the globe, or the remarks by artists or presidents about who is in or who is out. Or the hate and conspiracy theories which are experiencing a golden age online.

* * *

Based on Girard's theory, we have taken a critical look at our human striving for status. We have seen that competition and rivalry are fueled in various ways, in the economy or in the media. Various inner circles are being broken down, one might say, and replaced by one all-encompassing circle, and it is up to you to make sure you are in it. Instead of being part of a community, we become part of a mass. Of course, this process did not start with the introduction of social media. Spanish writer Ortega y Gasset lamented in the 1930s that his country was being populated by average people, enveloped by a soulless blandness, who only care about rest, food, and drink. Like spoiled children, who let their desires run free, but are grateful to no one for it. The average individual does not think for himself, said Ortega, but wants most of all to be like the other. They are stopped by nothing while the state inflames their desires,

making them believe they are entitled to have everything and impose their opinion on anyone, while full of resentment against all
who have more than them.[4] A century after Ortega, he has proven
right.

Dissatisfaction may also turn inwards. In a time of social
media and globalization, we can be absorbed more easily by the
homogenous crowd. But this may come paired with a worsening
self-image. Many cling on to that, since if you are a victim, at least
you know that you are *someone.*

It is a great paradox. In a society that has more means at its
disposal for connection than ever before, growing numbers of
people belong to nothing. Different studies across the Western
world show that two or three in every ten people always or often
feel lonely or lack meaningful relationships.

* * *

In the domain of love, too, relationships are taking on an increasingly conditional character. We want our partner to make us happy,
make us live up to our potential, be romantic, ideal, and exciting
in bed. If those are our criteria, it is difficult to show commitment
when a potential candidate comes by who seems to live up to that
standard better. Even though research indicates that partners who
remain loyal, even through tough times, are in the long-term (and
this is on average of course) happier, more satisfied, and healthier.

I am worried that there is a new generation of people aris-
ing who, more than other generations before them, are looking for
social contact, but are less capable than ever of commitment and a
safe attachment to the people around them. Progressive optimists
who find this old-fashioned complaining are more than welcome
to join me on a round in my neighbourhood, to visit the youth
here, the immigrants, and what I call the redundant class. The government is pumping millions into it to improve schooling, health,
and security. But they are oblivious to one phenomenon, and that
is the crisis of families.

4. Ortega y Gasset, *The Revolt of the Masses.* Still relevant.

I: THE PROMISES OF HYPERREALITY

According to estimates, half of the children in my neighbourhood see their father leave them at some point in their lives. This will likely not be much better in neighbourhoods in America and the rest of the Western world. As British psychiatrist Theodore Dalrymple wrote: there are more children with a television (or gaming computer for that matter) in their room than a father in their house. This is not conducive to safe attachment. A vicious aftereffect can be found in the official statistics, at least in my country: the odds of someone divorcing their partner is twice as high if one of those partners is the child of divorced parents. The odds of divorce are even thrice as big if both partners have divorced parents. In short: divorce trickles down through generations. We celebrate the freedom we have attained since the sexual revolution, but its price is being paid mostly by the poor who see the one thing they have crumble: family.

We should not forget however that many accomplished people too are susceptible to dissatisfaction and resentment. There is a widespread feeling of being run short. Resentment of Muslims against Westerners, of the white working class against foreigners, of conservatives against liberals. The resentment towards bankers, social service workers, the rich, politicians or Jews. Or just towards friends who have the ideal physique or colleagues who earn more than us.

Hyperreality promises us that we will belong if we are cool and authentic, if we are successful and have plenty of contacts. Hyperreality also promises us that we are social, immortal, and original, even though we might feel increasingly estranged from our surroundings. In a world without borders and limits, in which we can do what we want and will not be stopped by anyone from achieving self-actualization and status, it has become much harder to find a community to which we really belong.

II

THE MACHINE

6

Powers Unleashed

*How the promises reinforce each other,
how even sex becomes hyperreal,
and how we can unleash forces
without conscious choice.*

SO FAR, MY ANALYSIS might suggest that I am a grumpy pessimist who longs for the past, when the air was still clean and the sheep were still fat. This is not the case. I don't believe that everything only gets worse. I do, however, believe we are creating dangerous monsters which we neglect at our peril. The aim of this book has been allowing us to face this reality.

First, we found that a world exists which we might describe as hyperreality. We live in a world that is increasingly technological in nature, which is presented to us as an improved version of reality, in which we are not bound by normal limitations. This new world promises us satisfaction of all our desires.

Next, we saw that these promises are not fulfilled. Instead of satisfying our needs, hyperreality inflames them. Our desires will not be satisfied through more and more choice or opportunity because our desires are dynamic: they increase as choice does. Not only are our desires not satisfied, the instruments we put our trust in to help us satisfy them even start to carve out their own paths, leading to dangerous cliff edges. They set in motion different mechanisms that are very hard to stop. Eventually, this poses a risk to exactly those things we need to provide for our real human needs.

The first of these needs is material security, or wealth. Accumulate money and you will gain wealth: such is the creed of hyperreality. But when you give space to this desire for money, it may evolve and strengthen itself into a system in which money starts to become an end in and of itself. Note how the original goal, wealth, is increasingly defined in material terms. Eventually this goal is becoming eclipsed by purchasing power, profit, or even just the performance of the bond market. Without us noticing, we are undermining our true wealth by exhausting ourselves and the natural world around us.

Second, security. Take control, we are told, and you will be safe. But give too much space to this desire for control, and again it becomes an end instead of a means. It turns out that control too wants just one thing: more control. Our perception of "security" will eventually narrow, just as wealth did, to nothing than more control. Our supposed control will turn out to control us, which can ultimately be very dangerous.

Third, relationships. Improve your status, and you will belong. Again, the desire for status and recognition will become more important than the goal. The meaning of words like *relationship* and *belonging* narrows to nothing more than recognition, status, or your number of contacts, connections and likes. It may seem less like a system than the above two examples, but it is a dynamic that may mislead us in a variety of ways. Yet, it is interwoven with systems, such as the competitive economy or social media, which mould us into masses for whom social relations are mostly interesting economically. But the big question is whether this fake version of community hollows out or eclipses the real thing, leaving us in the end behind with nothing real to belong to.

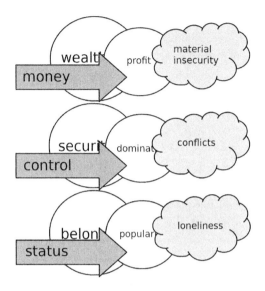

How the promises of hyperreality first narrow our goals and ultimately undermine our needs

I have approached this question mostly from the perspective of our desire, but we could just as easily consider it from the perspective of our anxieties. Precisely because we, as human beings, have important needs, we are susceptible to fear that we won't get enough of what we want. And when we become afraid, we become more open to superficial solutions.

* * *

I cannot finish without spending a few words on another very important human desire: sex. I have not talked about this before, since sexual desire functions very differently from the other desires we have already explored. The desires thus far have all been focussed on acquiring means to satisfy a certain need. Sexual desire is different: in essence, I believe, it is a desire oriented towards unity with someone, towards mutual acknowledgement. Moreover, it is willing to risk all means, all calculations, everything. Sex has dethroned kings and destroyed empires. It is quite understandable that sexual liberation during the sixties was seen by many as a movement of hope, a chance to finally be freed from a repressive system, just as it was among the revolutionaries in Paris before 1789. Sex is considered the apex of freedom, the antirational force *par excellence* against the process of becoming boring, uniform, tie-wearing slaves of the system.

And yet we can imagine a similar process in motion to those outlined above. With sex, too, hyperreality promises us a shortcut towards satisfaction. Take, for example, pornography, which is the ultimate hyperreality. Using technology, it skips all intermediate steps to arouse and satisfy the viewer immediately. But there is always a dividing line, a border: the screen. Strangely enough, this does not simply alienate one from others, but also from the self. Since erotic arousal is so easy to create, other senses no longer have a role to play. A deep satisfaction and a rich sexual experience become increasingly more difficult.

Porn is as old as the hills. Whoever has visited the ruins of Pompeii, for example, knows there is a good number of penises chalked on its walls. Still, these images are incomparable to the pornography in its varying degrees of rancidity which we can consume whenever we want with our glorious 5G connection. A huge number of boys and girls at the beginning of their sexual awakening have watched an anal penetration before they have seen the naked skin of one of their peers (this is not my personal observation, this is what researchers find). In mere seconds, we can make our deepest and wildest sexual fantasies appear on our screens, in multiple tabs at the same time. Faces are barely visible. Most of the time men and women are not portrayed as equals. A woman's body is the means to a certain end: the male orgasm. Similarly, men are objectified, as if they were animals subjected to their sexual instincts. For an entire generation of both boys and girls, this is the sexual education they take with them to bed.

This "pornographic sexual script" is not only found on 18+ websites. It permeates the media landscape. It has become cool and fashionable. Young boys and girls dress like porn stars, if only to make their profile pictures as attractive as possible. This does not only reaffirm patterns in which people consider each other to be objects, it also makes it more difficult to have deep, fulfilling, and intimate relations with a love partner or with any one. Research indicates that people who watch more pornography are less content, not only with their love life, but even with their sex life. And there is a very clear causal relationship between the consumption of pornography and adultery and divorce.

We are often told that our culture is oversexed. But strangely enough, real sex is hard to find in this age of pornography. Sexuality as an important and deep human activity is strikingly absent, says American feminist and media activist Jean Kilbourne.

> Men and women in music videos use each other. It is a cold and oddly passionless sex that surrounds us. A sense of joy is also absent; the people involved often look either hostile or bored. The real obscenity is the reduction of people to objects. Our culture is sex-crazed and sex-saturated, but strangely not erotic . . . . These sexual images aren't intended to sell our children on sex—they are intended to sell them on shopping. This is the intent of the marketers—but an unintended consequence is the effect these images have on real sexual desire and real lives.[1]

And so, sex, too, is eventually colonized by hyperreality.

* * *

An important question to ask ourselves is whether humans in the past were different. I do not think so. Perhaps they were even worse. The boozing and lovemaking nobility of the Middle Ages or the Roman emperors with their extravagant orgies were as much about money, power, and status. They too lived in their inebriating

---

1. Kilbourne, "So Sexy So Soon", 1-2.

ivory towers. Then too, people saw others as objects, then too hunger and exploitation roamed free through villages and slums.

But one thing is definitely new: we have much more powerful means to change the world according to our liking, not only for the elite but for the masses too. We really are working on realising our hyperreality. We really are now capable of building a world that permanently satisfies us. Our power to change the world, with all the consequences, is bigger than ever, as is our power to appease ourselves with feelings of satisfaction.

Many might argue that I am presenting too grim a vision. Indeed, do we not have more wealth, real security, and a society in which we can be ourselves? I would not want to change places with primitive societies in which large swathes of children (and women) died at birth. Thanks to our wealth and knowledge about hygiene there has been a dramatic decline in maternal and child mortality. Medicine has radically changed the world. We may be critical of progress, but it is probably fair to say that we all prefer anaesthetics in our blood to treat an inflamed molar rather than a club to the head.

In the domain of security, we can see progress as well. Consider the continuing decrease in violence in our societies. American anthropologist Steven Pinker has calculated that, despite the atrocities of the world wars, Nazism, and communism, the twentieth century has witnessed relatively fewer wars and murders than any preceding century. This is due to the exceptionally peaceful second half of the century.[2] What Pinker underestimates, according to me, is the possibility that this progress is due to the exceptional economic growth, which postpones conflict but which cannot continue indefinitely. What he is right about, though, is that some forms of violence which used to be normal are no longer accepted. Arguably, no one is of the opinion it is okay to kill criminals and foreigners, or to steal land simply because you are stronger. It still happens, but even the perpetrators try to deny it, while in the olden days there would be no need to do so.[3]

2. Pinker, *Better Angels.*

3. The annoying thing with Pinker is his belief that any progress and

When it comes to community and relationships, there has also been a revolution in what we think of as the rule of law. This is unique in the history of humanity. Equal treatment is deeply entrenched in our legislation. If we feel treated unfairly by the authorities, whether they be a police officer or a politician, an independent judge will hear our arguments. This enables a free society, for which I am grateful. This has to do with the fact that humans have learned to transcend their small communities, and to acknowledge that we are all connected to every other human being.

The issue at hand is not that we do not have wealth, security, or community. Rather, we have to realize that these great achievements are interwoven with dangerous mechanisms that pollute the source from which these revolutions came from. In fact, even what we call wealth can be both a result of virtues—for example, working together in a just and fair company—and by vices—like colonising others and exploiting their resources. It is quite possible that the unhealthy forces will overtake the healthy ones.

I believe this is exactly what is happening now. Many innovations in the West have been made possible because its culture had a deep respect for human integrity and liberty, precisely because limiting systems were being torn down! Simultaneously, however, this also eroded the limitations and boundaries of our desires. They have attained the space to grow. By breaking down one freedom-limiting system, we have sown the seeds of another. We have invoked forces we do not control: our wealth is more and more centred around money, our security on systems of control, and our society on competing, individualized masses.

---

improvement only became possible by shaking off our traditional Christian biases and superstitions. Nothing is further from the truth, I think. Charles Taylor, for example, shows in *A Secular Age* that secular thinking only became possible after Christianity. More recently historian Tom Holland wrote about this in *Dominion: How the Christian Revolution Remade the World*. He traces back the history of liberal values and discovers, to his own surprise, that they wouldn't have developed (or been discovered) were it not for the Christian faith. See also Girard, *Things Hidden*..

II: THE MACHINE

In the short run, these forces actually strengthen "progress". Since capital has gained so much room to manouvre over the past century, there has been enough growth to alleviate conflict in society. Because communities have increasingly withered away and people are individually competing with each other, there has been an enormous drive to innovate. But what if the pie can no longer grow? Purchasing power cannot grow if we no longer have access to cheap money and oil, or if our bodies and communities are exhausted. Our desire for more cannot be satiated once there are no more fish or forests. And what if healthy families in which children can grow up safely are becoming a rarity because we are no longer able to maintain our relationships? How will this affect morality, human liberty and dignity, which have been precisely the source of much of our progress? In short, collectively we have unleashed awesome forces, even though we did not consciously plan to do so.

Of course, we can point our finger towards bad people: fat cats who will do anything for money, political or technological or commercial elites who are not interested in real people. There are powers that be who have vested interests in the current system. However, we built this system together. The powers would not have power if we jumped off their bandwagon. This is the problem ahead: a world full of decent and civilized people, collectively messing things up in a decent and civilized fashion. The system is the problem, but it is a system we are all upholding.

This is one of the most important issues of our time, yet we are hardly giving it our attention. According to the French sociologist Jacques Ellul, who lived in the previous century, this is because the force we have unleashed fills us with awe. This force is above all criticism. This force is technique.

7

The Technological System

*How technology has become an autonomous
system with its own agenda,
according to Jacques Ellul.*

MAN HAS ALWAYS BEEN a technical being. Men and women have
always used tools—hammers, pencils, machines and other inventions—to achieve what they had in mind. But it was not until quite
recently that something fundamental changed. The grandparents
of our grandparents would be struck with amazement, if not terror, by what they saw if they could visit us and walk around in
our streets, or try to buy some food and cook a meal. Something
has changed: not in the tools that we use, but in the air that we
breathe and the environment that we live in. Our milieu has become technological.

The word technological needs clarification. The French thinker Jacques Ellul preferred the word *Technique*, with a capital T, by
which he didn't mean a certain tool or technology but a whole new
way of thinking. Our forefathers used tools in an environment that

was mainly shaped by natural and social forces and was limited by ideas about what is good or ethical or sacred. Our environment, on the contrary, is shaped and defined by technological forces.

After the nuclear bomb on Hiroshima, Japan declared solemnly that the emperor is not God, says Ellul. This is an example of how *Technique* dethrones all what was held sacred in the past. However, *Technique* only displaces gods in order to take their place. We will always have a natural feeling of awe towards a power that is bigger than us, be it the sun, the mountain or the emperor, so when the old power is sent to the museum of Ancient History, we will shift our awe to the new power, the power that seems to give us wealth, security and belonging, the power that seems to deliver progress and freedom. Nowadays this power is technology.

I find Ellul's writing key to understanding what what exactly is happening and what is good or dangerous about it.[1] Ellul lived from 1912 to 1994 in France, in the southern village of Pessac, close to the university of Bordeaux where he taught. He wrote more than fifty books about technology, power and freedom, in a time of great social change. His book *The Technological Society* impressed a whole generation of social critics when it was published in the US in 1964.

Ellul didn't want to be a philosopher. He always stressed the need to be rooted, to have feet in the mud, instead of living in hyperreal theoretical constructions. In 1951 he wrote:

> We must not think about Man, but of my neighbor Mario. I refuse to believe in the "progress" of humanity, when I see from year to year the lowering of standards among men I know, whose lives I follow, in the midst of whom I live—when I see how they lose their sense of responsibility, the seriousness in work, their recognition of a true authority, their desire for a decent life—[. . .] when I see them engaged in a desperate struggle, which

---

1. Ellul has written more than fifty books and it's impossible to summarize him here. A very good introduction to his thought is a series of interviews he gave on the Canadian radio, posthumously published as Ellul and Vanderburg, *Perspectives on Our Age*.

comes from the depths of their being, against something they don't know.[2]

A lot of techno-philosophers dismiss Ellul as a romantic, conservative pessimist, but often that's the result of misunderstanding his way of thinking. When you read his books you are struck by the actuality and fresh insights into modern phenomena. It's hard to put him in a box. He was a law scholar, historian, sociologist and theologian. He was a very active member of the *Résistance* during the war. Later he became one of the founding fathers of the French environmental movement, with his motto "think global, act local" and called himself an anarchist. He was inspired by Marx but he resisted communism. He spent his time with juvenile delinquents, when society was still thinking about this group in terms of jailing. He didn't want to adapt them to society, but wanted to redirect their "wrong maladaptation" to a "good maladaptation". He was a Christian and together with his wife led a small French reformed parish. He transcended a lot of different boxes.

The core of his critique of society is that our freedom is being undermined because technological systems have become autonomous. He talks about the mechanisms that I have described so far, and explains how every one of them is connected to each other by a common drive: the increase of means. This is what he calls *Technique*, which is not so much a certain technology as a whole social system that is rationally pressing onward towards more efficiency, more means, in every sphere, not only science and technology but also politics, economics, psychology and all other areas of our lives. The result of this is only judged by one criterion: does it give us more (speed, money, precision, stuff)? Then it is declared to be good, Ellul says.

Men have always used techniques, which are just ways to create more means in order to act. The hammer is a technique, but military planning is also a technique, as is a certain scientific method. The new thing in our times is that single techniques have been lifted out of their local context. They interact with each other

2. Ellul, *Presence*, 121.

and form a system, which Ellul calls "the technological phenomenon". Our society "is becoming purely technological . . . that is to say that in it one is exclusively preoccupied with the absolutely best means of attaining a certain end . . . one doesn't seek the good, but the efficient."[3]

> Technical civilization means that our civilization is constructed *by* technique, *for* technique, and *is* exclusively technique . . . herein lies the inversion we are witnessing. Without exception in the course of history, technique belonged to a civilization and was merely a single element among a host of nontechnical activities. Today technique has taken over the whole of civilization.[4]

An example. Scientists have done a lot of research to improve production methods for the car industry, which can now produce much faster cars for less money, enabling more people to buy a car of their own. This development has been ambiguous, however. The traffic also leads to more congestion and more accidents, for which traffic rules have had to be harmonized and enforced by a more efficient police. This is only possible with an efficient tax system, for which you need to build up a strong bureaucracy. But the dependence on cars is also one of the main reasons for governments to invest heavily in the energy supply from the Middle East, even if they have to build armies for that and even if they have to create support for these armies using a wide arsenal of propaganda and marketing techniques.

This is just one example of how this "technological system", this striving towards more means, more efficiency, and more organization, has its own built-in drive to expand. It is autonomous, claims Ellul, since it is expanding without a crooked elite behind the steering wheel. We have seen a few other examples already, like smart borders in the EU, or the financial markets. There is no ruler who explicitly decides that it is good, but it it nevertheless expands by itself. The technological system is always pressing towards control and order. But this only works if people adapt themselves to it.

3. Ellul, "L'Eglise et la vie économique". 25-26.
4. Ellul, *La Technique*, 128.

And that's where it hurts for Ellul. It becomes harder and harder for people to say no. Their culture, their community, their natural environment, their freedom: everything is molded to fit into technological society.

Yet the conflict remains. People and their cultures can never be fully adapted to a technological society. The more society is shaped and dominated by *Technique*, the more friction there will be: under the surface it will manifest as depression, unemployment or ecological disaster. Or the tension between the derivatives market and the real economy, a tension Ellul was early to predict, or the tension between rich and poor that would erupt in the form of terrorism. So on the one hand the technological system will expand, because that is its main goal; but on the other the costs and the risks will increase just the same.

No later than 1954 (!) when he wrote his manuscript for *The Technological Society* Ellul warned of the possibility that the technocratic state could become a totalitarian power gobbling up civil life. Totalitarian doesn't mean torture or terror. On the contrary:

> The police no longer carry out raids and there is nothing mysterious about them; therefore they are not felt to be oppressive. Police work has become "scientific". Their files contain dossiers of every citizen. The police are in a position to lay hands on anyone "wanted" at any moment, and this obviates to a great degree the necessity of doing so. No one can evade the police or disappear. But then, no one wants to. An electronic dossier is not particularly fearsome. [It is the job of the technician to develop human techniques] to such a pitch of perfection that even the man face to face with the perfectly functioning machine no longer has human initiative or the desire to escape. The ability to forget the machine is the ideal of technical perfection.[5]

* * *

5. Ellul, *The Technological Society*, 413.

Many people take offense at this language. Why criticize something so amazing and beautiful as technology? How dare he! Doesn't technology help us to live a good life, without poverty, without the hard labor of washing clothes by hand every night or ploughing the earth with horse power under the scorching sun? Yes, that is true: we can use technology for good, and we have in fact always done, even the washboard and the horse plough were advanced technologies at the time. Man is a technological being: technology is in fact an extension of man. But it is an extension of a certain aspect of man, an aspect that should be balanced with others. At the moment we are extending and enlarging one aspect of our being and attaching all our dreams and notions of progress to it. As a consequence, says Ellul, we are driving at tremendous speed—to go nowhere.

Some years ago I had the chance to talk to the well-known Californian technology guru Kevin Kelly about his book *What Technology Wants*. Kelly is co-founder of *Wired Magazine* and a famous tech-lover. His analysis is quite close to Ellul's: technology has become a system with its own law and its own will even, and we can't stop it. Yet for Kelly this will is good. It stimulates creativity and creates diversity. This makes it nothing less than the next phase in the natural evolution of the cosmos.[6]

In essence technology is neutral, Kelly says, because it enables you to do good as well as evil. But, and that's why it sums up positively, it gives us choice we didn't have before. We are always able to choose to not use the technology if we would like. Every technological innovation leads to more choices, and so to more freedom, and so to a better world.

The cosmic vision of Kelly is thought-provoking. But about one phenomenon he doesn't write a word: power. I asked him about this. Isn't technology in essence power over something? What does power do with us? What does power in our hands do to our desires, and can we trust them? Don't our desires change if we get more means, more power? Kelly didn't have a clue. Power was

---

6. Kelly, *What Technology Wants.*.

too vague a concept, he said; he preferred to talk about freedom of choice.

Technology is the power to act. But power is always influencing our orientation, and as a consequence also the direction of our society. Technology is power, and as such it always interacts with the power relations that already exist. This doesn't make technology *a priori* good or bad, in theory, but in practice it always carries consequences which are never neutral. The techno-neutralism which is popular among philosophers wants to make a balance of directly good or harmful results, but this is superficial. All technologies can be used for good or bad, all powers can be used to do harm or to do good. But what we need to know is what this increasing power to do good and evil does with the underlying structure of society, with our relations. In philosophical terms: instead of techno-neutralism we need techno-structuralism.

Let's think about the technologies that we talked about, like money. Money is a technology. It is a way to transfer debt from one party to another. The dependency relation is an inherent aspect of the paper bill we use. This means we are making use of a power relationship. And this power will always be used in the end. If someone can not pay back what they owe, there will always be a party that has to bow to power, perhaps in the shape of a bailiff.

Kelly would say: money has positive and negative consequences, but it enriches us with choice since we can always choose not to use it, which makes the whole phenomenon essentially good. Herein lies his mistake. We usually don't have this choice. Money is a power relation, it changes the structure of society, it creates a situation by which you cannot do without anymore, which means it is not neutral. This doesn't make it impossible to use money for good. But neutral it isn't, and the freedom not to use it we haven't.

In the end Kelly assumes that our desires are good. But our desires are by nature mimetic, which means they are directed by the desires of the other, often in the shape of rivalry. We attempt to attain wealth, security and belonging by striving for money, control and status, but these phenomena are inseparable from the power of some people to dominate others. If we follow these desires we are not just neutrally expanding our possibilities of choice, but increasing the power of some over others.

Ellul himself doesn't concern himself with whether a certain technology is good or bad in essence, he only points to the consequence of the technological system for society. He is convinced that the technological system as a whole always leads to a concentration of power. In practice, economic and political actors always have to increase their means, to mitigate the risks of our age, to keep ahead of competitors, to pay off debts. There is no difference between capitalists and communists, between market and state. Both strive towards more means, more growth, more technology, to be able to organize better and stronger and to increase their impact and their power, so both have to obey the central law of the technological system, which is efficiency. When we claim these laws are neutral, deep inside we mean that they are good, because they give us power. And we stand in religious awe before this power.

* * *

Techniques have always existed as inseparable part of man, but the technological system is a modern phenomenon, a result of a certain worldview, a project with its roots in the Enlightenment. René Descartes regarded nature as a whole system of automatons who keep themselves going according to logical laws. Nature is a machine, just as understandable as clocks, he said. Whoever knows the laws can also use them. The enlightened man is "master and owner of nature", thought the famous philosopher. Plants and animals are things that can be manipulated to make them useful.

This usefulness, this utility, was what the other Enlightenment thinker Francis Bacon placed at the center of his worldview as the ultimate criterion for all our acts. Bacon is known as the man of knowledge. He believed that science and technology are an imitation of God's creation, and that progress will ultimately lead us to paradise. It is a paradise that doesn't revolve around God, but around man. According to Bacon nature has to be forced to serve man. Nature must be "taken by the forelock", grabbed by her hair, subdued, conquered, shaken, even "penetrated in her most intimate chambers".[7] Note the rape connotation! It's instructing to know why Bacon wanted us to act like this. Only in this way can we get the power to roll back the consequences of the Fall, he hoped. Science and technology have to manipulate the world in such way that it becomes good, irrespective of any bad inclinations man may have. In other words, we need a world where it doesn't matter if you make good or bad choices in practice, because the outcome will be good anyway. It is a good way to describe the motivation of many technicians, planners and politicians nowadays trying to solve the world problems with better organization. It is also a good way to define hyperreality.

7. Midgley, *Science as Salvation*, 78.

8

The Chicken Machine

*How the technological system leads us
step by step towards more efficiency
and homogeneity, in the direction of
an impossible brave new world.*

THE MASTERY OF NATURE is nowhere more visible than in agriculture. My own country, the Netherlands, is good at it. We are just a small country in Western Europe, but we are the second largest agricultural exporter in the world, after the US. To understand why and how this is possible I visited different companies in this sector, to talk to farmers and developers about the knowledge and technology that made them so competitive. One of the companies I visited was a so-called hatchery, which gave me a sneak preview into the future of agriculture—and maybe of society as a whole.

I expected something like a farm, with straw and chicken and the smell of animals, but reality was different. A hatchery is a factory. This one was a building with 22 permanent incubators, filled with 57,600 eggs each, hatching chicks at the right temperature in exactly 21 days. A continuous stream of freshly hatched yellow fluff balls, just waking up to a strange world and feeling their legs for the first time, are taken by a conveyor belt across the building to a counting machine, on the other side of which they were sprayed into crates with exactly a hundred chicks each. Every week, 1.6 million of them are transported to poultry farms. After growing 60 grams daily for 42 days, they reach the perfect weight to be cut up, sold and thrown in the pan.

Broiler companies find themselves engaged in a fight for the most efficient method and the most efficient chicken. As a trade magazine said: a chicken is "nothing more than an efficient converting machine" which converts soy into chicken breasts. There are different companies that dominate the market, but among the chicken at least there's a clear winner: the Ross 308, which is selected, crossbred, and cultivated to grow as fast as possible. All broilers want this one. The Ross 308 by far outperforms other breeds, which is why 95 percent of all broilers in the Netherlands are of that type. Others have nearly disappeared.

Farmers, too, have disappeared. There are barely ten significant hatcheries in the Netherlands. The competition is relentless, I was told by the director of the hatchery. Their turnover is 240 million Euros, and yet the margins are so slim that he barely breaks even. The risks are enormous. If the market slows down briefly, it ruins his company. A disease outbreak, such as avian flu, is another risk. In that scenario, it is most economical for the sector to preventatively cull a couple million chickens, but for the individual hatchery it can be fatal.

Civil society organizations are critical of this "powerchicken", which is too heavy to stand on its own legs and needs a boatload of antibiotics to prevent disease outbreak in the hatcheries. So who is in a position to change this situation? The hatchery is not. Neither is the breeder or the butcher. It is no surprise that they are often cynical about campaigns run by "left-wing" do-gooders. If they do not produce their product in the most efficient way possible, they will be outplayed by the international market.

Not more than forty employees work in the hatchery. The computer is in charge. This place has nothing in common with a farm; it is a white windowless building with the only vegetation around being a fig tree in the head office. Everything is sterile. The winners in this sector are the machine makers. This is what the Dutch export is really about. What the Dutch sell worldwide is not so much chicken, but feed-fuelled, machine created edible chicken legs, millions a day, and the accompanying technologies. It's vastly cheaper and more efficient than the old village farm.

The lens of efficiency never looks far ahead. When I visit people in the sector, I always ask them what they think the farm sector will look like in the future, but no one knows. "Less labour", "more robots", "a bigger stable", "more production", they offer. Some variation of "more efficient" is always the answer from everyone: farmers, salesmen, researchers, policy makers or bankers. Which means ultimately that nobody is really questioning the path we are following, towards a big food machine where nutrients are converted into as perfect as possible "food products", in multi-storeyed factories where tens of millions of chickens are crammed into a few acres to be grown into chicken breasts in 42 days, under the skillful management of robots and one employee behind a screen.

What does this do to flavour, to our health? What does it do to farms and to our relation with nature? Technicians trust that future technologies will make these questions obsolete. To build a healthy diet, for example, you can sell carrots ready-to-eat and prescraped. People will buy that. They are even sold as a healthy nutrient in a powdered form, for fifty euros per pot. One company has even gone a step further. In these artificial times, people do not like broccoli anymore. This is a shame, since broccoli contains a lot of glucosinolates, which are a good protection against cancer. So they have invented what they call "super broccoli"; broccoli powder with added proteins that trick people who dislike broccoli into eating it. Hyperreal broccoli, so to say.

The global food machine will be incredibly cost-efficient, when it comes to costs that can be expressed in monetary terms.

But many costs (for instance loss of capital supplies, as we saw in chapter 3) cannot be expressed in these terms and hence will be passed on to others, like distant people who see their forest disappear, or to the next generation who will inherit depleted fish stocks or poorer soils.

Farmers too will disappear. What will this mean for poorer countries with large rural populations? They will have to get used to ever-growing cities and slums. While most economists do not dare speak it out loud, the technological system is creating a huge class of "obsolete" people, not useful anymore for the growing dynamic urban society.

* * *

Efficiency gives us more productivity, but there is always a trade-off. We all know the examples of our own lives: the reorganizations our managers imposed on the workplace, in which a certain model of organization was more important than knowledge about the work you were doing. Or the swamp you got sucked into when your tax returns were not correct and you tried to get the right person on the phone who couldn't do anything because the computer said no. Or that moment you took the family to the beach by bus but the checkout chip reader didn't function properly, a fact you only discovered at night, when you were not allowed to enter the bus home because apparently you were out of credit.

These are all features, says Ellul, of Technique; a technical system that forces us to adapt to it. It was not without reason that we started with agriculture, because it very well illustrates one of the most important characteristics of the technical system: it is a homogenizing force. Put differently, because it looks only for efficiency, it always moves towards monoculture. Yet, this comes with a price.

Look, for example, to the opposite: a complex system such as a tropical rainforest. Within a forest plants, animals, matter, and energy all have their own role to play. The health of this ecosystem cannot be measured by looking to production only, by the amount of timber produced or the amount of carbon stored. Rather, it is about the viability of the whole, the ability to regenerate after a drought or a tree disease. This is what ecologists call resilience. A rainforest is not very "productive"; it's not an efficient way to grow a certain crop or tree, and it's hard to harvest, but it is *resilient*. In general, this resilience increases when diversity and variety in species, genes and interlinkages increases. The more diversity, the stronger the ecosystem.

Monocultures are much more efficient than a rainforest, in terms of production. Yet they are much more vulnerable. Vast stretches of land populated by a single genetically modified type of cotton can be incredibly productive. But a single new kind of fungus or too intense a rainy season can make the system collapse—along with the livelihoods of numerous farmers. A rainforest, on the other hand, can persist for millions of years, its diversity enabling it to continuously adapt to changing circumstances. It is resilient.

But this cannot feed a growing population. Therefore we have to stake everything on growth and production; in other words, on efficiency. We have changed a diverse and local agriculture into a global monoculture. According to the UN Food and Agriculture Organization, over the past century the genetic diversity of agricultural crops has shrunk by a quarter. Just twelve crops and fourteen animal species make up 80 percent of all food on earth. The variation within that diversity of crops and species is also declining. This is called genetic erosion.

In an economic sense the diversity, and hence resilience, of farmers is diminishing as well. To be able to make the necessary investments, in pesticides, fertilizer, machinery, or seeds, they have to take out more loans. They become dependent on a small group of players who have access to the capital the farmers need. Six multinationals control as much as 60 percent of the seed market and 75 percent of the agrochemical market.

But is not the same happening on a cultural level? Traditional forms of knowledge and experience are disappearing. The more technical and intensive agriculture becomes, the fewer jobs it creates and the more people move to the cities. One day I went to a conference organized by The Economist and sponsored by Monsanto about how to "feed the world". During lunch they served nice organic vegetables. But among hundreds of participants and panelists I didn't see more than two farmers and two people from the South. Panellists talked about the need for more efficiency, better transport and equipment, and how to "explain" to farmers what the world needs. The message was clear: farmers are obstacles on the path towards a productive and efficient global food machine.

In reality, we will never get to this endpoint of the perfect, efficient world food system, since with every step we lose resilience to cope with diseases or trade wars or climate change or all the other difficulties that reality imposes on us. Yet, for now, it is the path our agriculture ministries, advisers, researchers and banks are following. It shows us clearly what the technological system as a whole wants to do with our life. We get ever more production, but lose resilience.

* * *

It is clear now that *Technique* is not simply a certain technology or a machine. As Ellul writes, the machine is in fact the *ideal* of technique. The technical system tends to change the world into a machine, not only in agriculture but also economics, the money market, politics and even mankind itself. The various different promises of hyperreality push us in the direction of a concentrated, monocultural system, in which in the end only the output matters. This is not the result of our conscious choice. Rather, it is the consequence of the path we follow, with its own laws. The technological system considers our culture, diversity, suboptimal farmers, irrational feelings, and so on, to be obstacles on our glorious path towards a world without want.

The machine doesn't search for what is meaningful, or good, but what is *useful*. But useful for what? That becomes less and less clear in an ever more useful world. In the words of Ellul:

> Today everything has become "means." There is no longer an "end;" we do not know whither we are going. We have forgotten our collective ends, and we possess great

means: we set huge machines in motion in order to arrive nowhere.

Thus man—who used to be the end of this whole humanist system of means—man, who is still proclaimed as an "end" in political speeches, has in reality himself become the "means" of the very means which ought to serve him: as, for instance, in economics or the State.

This remarkable proliferation of means thus leads to making everything "useful." In our world everything has to serve: that is to say, to be a "means." Art and everything that is "useless" has to give way to the necessity for "utility." Anything that does not serve some purpose must be eliminated or rejected.[1]

The only agenda of the technical system is the multiplication of the means. It wants but one thing: progress. It wants to know every star and every pathway in the Amazon rainforest. It wants to make crime disappear, and have no school kid ever bump their head. It wants to chart and patent all plant and animal species, and preferably our relationships too. It wants to colonize Mars and eradicate all disease.

* * *

The machine also takes on the human race itself. Humans could be so much healthier and stronger, more stable and happier. Human characteristics are increasingly addressed as problems that need to be solved. A new approach in this respect is so-called gamification. "Reality doesn't motivate us effectively," a game researcher at a progressive university writes. "Reality isn't engineered to maximize our potential. Reality wasn't designed from the bottom up to make us happy."[2] So if we were given the chance to to get points, stickers, rewards or other incentives on our phones for improving our behavior, going out to vote, taking on a sustainable lifestyle, and signing petitions to denounce exploitation in the fashion industry, the world could be much better, and fun too.

1. Ellul, *Presence*, 63.
2. McGonigal, *Reality Is Broken*, 121.

This brings us all the way back to where this book started: hyperreality. Hyperreality is the showroom of the technical-economic system that wants to improve the world by turning it into a controllable machine, a "happiness machine". It lays a filter over nature that is smooth and frictionless. We become a global Dubai: a dream city in the desert, hosting nothing but successful young people, surrounded by glass skyscrapers, and perfect artificial beaches. A city that can only exist, however, by trading oil, taking over farms in Africa, and flying in cheap Asians to do the cleaning.

This happiness machine is a utopian project. It will never be able to abolish the boundaries of reality. Moreover, it parasitizes on this reality, something which can not go on forever. Yet for now, we maintain our belief in hyperreality and allow it space to expand ever more.

The machine has to be automated; that is much cheaper and more efficient. From dairy farmers to bookstores, from cleaners to caregivers, if any of them can be replaced by technology, they will. Even the military will be obsolete one day. The policymakers of the US Air Force want a fully autonomous fleet operational in 20 years, constituted by unmanned aerial vehicles that cannot only shoot targets themselves, but even make the decision whether to shoot or not as well. Robots are much more efficient at decision-making than humans, the researchers say, with the added benefit of not getting post-traumatic stress disorder.

The idea that robots could get that much power scares people. But there is one thing even scarier than robots: people behaving like robots. Politicians who only approve plans that increase economic efficiency, or talk shows who choose their guests on the basis of calculations of viewing behaviour, or people who let Amazon or Google decide what they should buy next or what restaurant to visit. By collecting, indexing, and making transparent all knowledge in the world, the technological system promises to optimize everything in our lives.

Everything is being optimized, catered specifically to me. What interests are behind it, who pays for what—all that is invisible because, in the end, I am the centre of hyperreality. *Me and my desires.* If efficiency is the only criterion for this machine, then my innermost instincts will be decisive. And my innermost instincts are those of an infant: they perceive of the world as scary and cold and only want warmth, safety, and food. As long as it is comfortable.

At least that is what Aldous Huxley foresaw in his dystopian book *Brave New World,* in 1931. It's a world which revolves around production and comfort, where everyone is conditioned to belong to a certain caste, and where every unhappy feeling is solved by swallowing a medicine called soma. At the end of the book there is an important discussion between Mustapha Mond, the governor of Western Europe, and a "savage", who was raised in nature and is shocked about what the world has become.

> "The world's stable now", Mond says. "People are happy; they get what they want, and they never want what they can't get. They're well off; they're safe; they're never ill; they're not afraid of death; they're blissfully ignorant of passion and old age; they're plagued with no mothers or fathers; they've got no wives, or children, or lovers to feel strongly about; they're so conditioned that they practically can't help behaving as they ought to behave."

Mond explains that, if anything unpleasant should somehow happen, there's always soma to give people a holiday from the facts.

> "In the past you could only accomplish these things by making a great effort and after years of hard moral training. Now, you swallow two or three half-gramme tablets, and there you are. Anybody can be virtuous now. You can carry at least half your morality about in a bottle. Christianity without tears—that's what soma is."

The savage replied with disgust:

> "But I like the inconveniences," he said.
> "We don't," said Mond. "We prefer to do things comfortably."
> "But I don't want comfort. I want God, I want poetry, I want real danger, I want freedom, I want goodness. I want sin."

"In fact," said Mustapha Mond, "you're claiming the right to be unhappy."

"All right then," said the Savage defiantly, "I'm claiming the right to be unhappy."

Mustapha Mond shrugged his shoulders. "You're welcome," he said.[3]

No one listens to the savage in the end. He ends up being no more than a strange voice from the past, incomprehensible for people who feel so happy that they never ponder going back to sin and virtue, bravery and morality, freedom and pain. History has ended.

Now I am sure that the book is a fantasy: we will never achieve the Brave New World. We will never be able to reduce the world to a machine. We will always push against the walls of nature and the laws of resilience, the irrational feelings of men and the anger of the poor. But for now we are heading towards Brave New World at warp speed and we let the technological system dictate our lives. As we have seen before, it is a power that takes our freedom. So it's time to turn our attention to power and freedom.

3. Huxley, *Brave New World*, Chapter 16.

III

DAZZLING FREEDOM

9

On Ends and Means

How Mahatma Gandhi restated the problem
in terms of ends and means,
which is ultimately a question of trust;
or in other words, faith.

ONCE UPON A TIME there was a man who signed a pact with the devil. So goes the legend that is told in different versions in different ages. The man was bored, fed up with his monotonous existence. He was called Faust. In order to achieve ultimate happiness he turned to magic—and the devil appeared. The devil offered him all knowledge and ultimate happiness, but on one condition: that the devil would take his soul at the very moment that he achieved it. Faust accepted the offer. He started to receive everything he ever had dreamed of. Fame, sex, power: he tried all of them in the different versions of the story. In Goethe's version he even got the power to print money. To cut things short, in the end Mr. Faust found real happiness and total satisfaction, but at that very moment the devil came to get him. He found everything that he desired, but he lost himself.

The story shows that it matters what power we invoke to reach a certain goal. The means we choose to find happiness and fulfillment are not irrelevant: on the contrary, they can ultimately undermine the end that we try to achieve. This is in line with my story until now, about a hyperreality promising everything but in the end undermining our freedom to find fulfillment. Restating this story in terms of ends and means will help us to discern where we go wrong and how we can choose something else. It will make clear that the crisis around us is not the result of bad organization but of trusting the wrong powers.[1]

* * *

When I traveled through India a few years ago, during a course organized by Indians to teach us about poverty, I had the chance to visit a house in Mumbai where Mahatma Gandhi lived, almost a century ago. It's a kind of museum now, and I don't remember much anymore but the burning heat on the streets of Mumbai, the fantastic paneer kofta that we ate at night and one very special sentence that was written on a small plate hanging humbly in the back of this house. The sentence read: "Ends and means are exchangeable." This sentence struck me, and I had to chew on it for a few years before discovering that this is the key to understanding politics.

It was an important principle of Gandhi, I discovered. He took it from Jesus's Sermon on the Mount. If peace is your end, violence can not be your means. If a loving society is your goal, competition cannot be your road to it. If real satisfaction is what you want, consumerism will not bring you there.

There is a very interesting biography online written by Gandhi himself, *Satyagraha in South Africa*, in which he looks back on his fight for civil rights as a lawyer in South Africa around the

---

1. The Dutch economist Bob Goudzwaard gave me some crucial insights for this chapter: see also the book he wrote with Vander Vennen and Van Heemst, *Hope in Troubled Times*.

year 1900. In this book he emphasizes time and again that truth and justice can only be our end if it is also our means. We are just the instruments of the "Almighty Will", he writes, that's why we often don't understand what helps or inhibits us. So we should be content with only knowing the means. "If they are pure, we can let the goal take care of itself without fear."[2]

Obviously that is easier said than done. Every ideology, if it be communism, capitalism or the wahabism from the Arabian desert, is deeply convinced that it is leading us towards a bright future of peace, prosperity, respect, harmony and cheap beef for everyone. So convinced, in fact, that its followers don't carefully choose the means, which makes the end slip away time and again. That's why it doesn't make a lot of sense to adhere to a certain school or party for its nice goals, because every school or party has nice goals. Even right-wing extremists long for peace, prosperity and a healthy community. Nice ideals. But usually, just like us, they don't dare to let the goal take care for itself, as Gandhi advised. They want the shortcut, which always leads over piles of corpses.

For the premodern mind, ends and means belonged together. That's what Aristotle taught: happiness is the good and virtuous life itself. In other words: you can't reach the good life with bad means. During modernity we have loosened the connection between ends and means. Science became a specialized department of thinkers who didn't want to bother themselves with what is good or evil. The Enlightened thinkers put all their focus on the right *method*. Not the *why*—what is good or bad—but the *how* became the subject of scientists. What to do with this knowledge, consecutively, was not their business.

With their technical and mathematical view on the world, modern people approach more and more things as instruments, as means. We learn to collect and multiply them in order to be able to secure our goals. The problems we create in the process will be solved later, if we have even more means. Aldous Huxley wrote about this phenomenon, even before his bestseller *Brave New World*, in a book titled *On Ends and Means*.

2. Gandhi, *Satyagraha in South Africa*.

All together this has brought us a society that is full of means but where it's hard to find goals for which to live. Everything we touch becomes an instrument, like King Midas who saw his world change into gold. A world consisting of only means, and no ends— that is another definition of a trance, a hyperreality where we float along as individual atoms, flooded with goods and images that satisfy desires that in reality are exactly the opposite of what we were actually looking for.

To be clear, the word *means* can have different meanings. A means is a road, a trajectory, the path we follow to reach a certain goal. But in plural it is also the things that we amass in modern times to get things done: for example knowledge, money, or power. They are means (things) but also the means (the way) that we trust will bring us to our ends.

Think again about money and growth. No economist would say economic growth is a goal in itself. It's a means to an end, to wealth and prosperity, of course. We have to grow because then. . . we can have better jobs, a better environment or peace between nations. Growth is no more than a necessary means. But then something dark happens. As soon as a means is considered necessary, it starts to narrow the mind. Step by step it changes our moral boundaries, but also the goal, very subtly. Instead of wealth in the broad sense we start to focus on wealth, in the narrow sense, on financial profit. Ultimately our goal will be eclipsed or narrowed to the point where the means, money, has taken the place of the goal. The means has become the end.

The same happens to security. When this important goal or need is threatened, we cling to the means that we deem necessary, only to discover in the end that our noble goal of security is eclipsed by instrumental goals like reducing risks or domination or even the thirst for control itself. The same also happens to our search for belonging. If we put all our trust in the means, in status or individual achievement, we will soon define our goals in ever narrower terms, to the point that we are finally ready to do everything for recognition, for success, for status, for popularity. The ends have been eclipsed by our means.

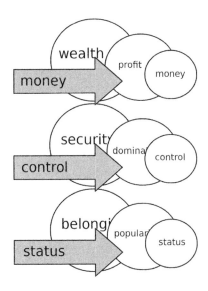

How means become ends in themselves

The narrowing of the mind by the systems we created ourselves looks suspiciously like the narrowing of the mind we see in "primitive" societies. Fear was central in primitive religion. In case of danger, people gave up part of their power to what they regarded as higher powers, idols, symbolized by a totem or an image. This led to worship, and norms and values were adapted in the process. The idol became the ultimate goal; the means took the drivers' seat. The whole tribe could collectively decide, after three bad harvests, that the shaman was right in ordering the crowd to bind your daughter to a pole, dance a prehistoric rumba and cut her throat in front of a big penis. That was called necessary, even virtuous, because otherwise the god would not give rain. Without rain, no prosperity. But you might wonder if it is prosperity when the next day you have rain, but your daughter has no head.

In our enlightened world we don't do such stupid things anymore. We don't believe in gods. But secretly we still pay homage to powers who decide how to structure our society. And those powers can have us under their spell. With all our rationalism we can still be under the influence of powers stronger than us. That's what we see most clearly in wartime, when countless people rally behind their leader unquestioningly and friends turn to monsters in a day. But we also see the powers reflected in the hope and fear politicians express for credit rating agencies, or in the awe and fear with which software developers talk about artificial intelligence.

We think we are so much smarter than the primitive mind, but the adjustment of our norms and values to the will of the powers can happen much more rationally and systematically compared to the simple gods of old. Their grasp has become total: totalitarian if you will. We have to cut back on social spending everywhere because the bond market threatens to become unstable. We have to roll out surveillance on every citizen since the terrorists are among us. We have to sell every mountain and every forest in order to safeguard our access to resources to sustain our standard of living, and for fear of other countries trying to catch up with our military might we have to spend a jaw-dropping amount of money to modernize our nuclear weapons. We don't want to use them, obviously, but we need more of them to force others to not use them either.

Are these gods really different from the gods that in biblical times were called idols? Is this real different from Mammon, the unjust god of money, the Baal, who was sculpted in the Middle East in the shape of a huge phallus, or Moloch, the god of war who demanded child sacrifices, gods that had whole civilizations in their grasp and who required or allowed them to carry out barbaric and grueling acts?

There is a connection between idols and images. As soon as we make an image of what we regard as authority, it becomes easier to reify and to absolutize it. Idols are images of a phenomenon that start to lead a life of their own and take power over us. It is no coincidence that the Ten Commandments warn against making images of God. This detour brings us back to hyperreality, because hyperreality is a world that is built with images. Instead of words, relationships and stories, we increasingly get our wisdom from images, be they news items, youtube clips or financial figures.

Images are unquestionable, penetrating and decisive for what we do and do not believe. But they also conceal that we might be losing exactly that which makes us human, which is our freedom to judge and to choose.[3]

This brings us to the area of religion. This is what we have already touched on in the chapter on money. According to theologian Lesslie Newbigin, religion is "that which has ultimate authority over a believer or a society, through norms and values or through models and patterns with which they evaluate and organize their experiences"[4]. So according to Newbigin the formal religion of people can be different from the religion that has ultimate authority over their thinking and their acting.

The images fired towards us every day on the real or virtual streets are images of the gods of our time: money, control and success, with all the lower gods who accompany them, like youth, health or sex. The technology that generously gives us all these riches is the supreme god, raised above every criticism. Sometimes I stand before a class or a group to talk about this, and to illustrate my point I break a smartphone in pieces. People react with disgust, they are really, really offended by this act. The smartphone gives us so much! The smartphone enables us to do good! Who am I to treat this savior, this hope for mankind, which enables us to share videos, to check the weather, to talk to friends, to access all the world's knowledge, so badly? The smartphone is looked upon with awe. The smartphone is holy. Of course I don't care about the smartphone itself so much as the passion with which people cling

3. A lot has been written about the relationship between idol and image, including by Ellul, in his book *The Humiliation of the Word*. Ellul makes a fundamental distinction between word and image. Words convey dialogue, meaning and relations, which all belong to the realm of "truth". Images convey (imagined) facts and certainties, which all belong to the realm of "reality". We need both word and image in our lives, he says, but when images dominate, as they clearly do in our times, truth is displaced by reality, by facts without meaning, which are easy to manipulate. It's no accident, he says, that the Bible talks about the God who speaks and forbids making images of him. Without words of truth we will get stuck in reality—or at least in the image of reality which is presented to us.

4. Newbigin, *Open Secret*, 160–61.

to it. It has become a symbol, the fetish of the god of technology, even though ultimately it's nothing more than a thing. (Which makes it all the more important to smash a smartphone in public now and then.)

Ultimately my prediction is that the gods will take off their masks and turn against us. In other words, if we don't watch out, we will gain the whole world, but lose our freedom. This means that this is not just an organizational challenge. It's a spiritual challenge, which cries for a spiritual answer.

10

The Spirituality of the Way

*How we find a possible way out
in the spirituality of Jesus,
for whom the end does not justify the means,
but vice versa.*

ONCE UPON A TIME, there was another man who was offered a deal by the devil. His name was not Faust, but Jesus. At the time it happened, he was in the desert of Judaea, to fast for forty days and contemplate the task that lay ahead of him. Jesus lived in a time of severe oppression. The Romans ruled the land with an iron fist. Shortly before Jesus' birth, Sepphoris, a city in Galilee, was completely crushed by the Romans. Its inhabitants were either crucified or sold as slaves. They were hard times, in which money, success, and power ravaged the world, not as efficiently and globally as they do now, yet all the more bloodily. Jesus' contemporaries chose varying responses, which are still recognizable in our times. Accept the system in order to improve it (Sadducees), try to remain pure and clean religiously (Pharisees), prepare for the day you can violently kick out the bad guys (Zealots), or go offline and feel zen in a retreat center (Essenes).

This Jesus went to the desert, and there the devil appeared before him, in the shape of three temptations. Three temptations that, at first glance, seem a bit strange and nonsensical. Why not make bread appear out of stones if you are hungry? Why not jump off a famous building to show everyone how cool you are? And why not accept reality, bow before evil, and gain all the power in the world?

What strikes me is that these temptations are linked to the three core needs of humans that we have discussed before. Material security, recognition, and a feeling of power and control. These three needs are the breeding ground for our desires for money, status, and power. What is wrong with eating? Or using your status to gain followers? Or trying acquire power? After all, you can do good with these things.[1]

Essentially Jesus is confronted with everything on which human history is built, namely that for good ends all means are justified. The means are a bit dirty, but you can do good things with them, right? It is history's big lie. Jesus knows this. He resolutely rejects it, always with the argument that he only listens to God. His answers are not very elaborate, he seems to arbitrarily quote a few verses from a single page from the Torah, which tells faithful Jews that you will only find prosperity and security if you hand over your life and follow the path of the God of freedom. Jesus does not choose fear.

---

1. We also come across the temptation of Christ in the fascinating story about the grand inquisitor in Dostoevsky's *The Brothers Karamazov*. When Jesus comes back on earth in medieval Spain, the grand inquisitor interrogates him and explains to him why the devil had it right: happiness for all can only be achieved when you use every means possible. Freedom has to be sacrificed along the way, it's the price we have to pay. People cannot handle freedom: what they want is bread, power, and mystery. Thinks the grand inquisitor.

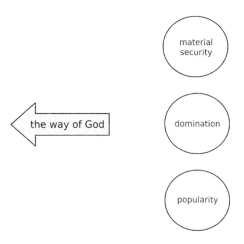

The three promises Jesus rejects

Some people may think it's not fitting to talk about spirituality at this moment in time, least of all Christian spirituality. Indeed, was it not the church that manifested itself so often throughout history as an oppressive power that ruled through fear? Yet, I want to discuss it, since I believe Jesus' spirituality was never intended to be a religion. It is meant to set us free from the powers that hold us in chains. And this can show us the way out of the machine, how unglorious this might be for people who'd rather pull ourselves out of the swamp by our own hair like Baron von Münchhausen did.

Besides, I believe that all of us, whether we call ourselves people of faith or not, are spiritual beings who have an ingrained inclination to put our trust in something, even if this is not the result of a rational deliberation. We all have our own methods, powers, means, people, or tricks, which we believe can help us achieve our goals, i.e. our needs. Hence I believe everyone has faith in something. Put simply, we have to discuss what kind of faith is healthy and what kind is not. And what that means for the means.

What we can learn from Jesus—who inspired Gandhi to formulate his ideas about ends and means—is that the end does not justify the means, regardless of how great and noble the end is. Rather, it is the other way around, the means justify the end. In fact, the sacred means, the sacred way, that is the starting point of the end itself. That is the seed, in the words of Jesus, for the kingdom of God, the world of shalom. Only in the future will it be fully grown, but it begins here, right in the heart of this violent world. It has its own principles, which come from a home far beyond our way of thinking. Instead of taking, it is about sharing. Instead of status, it is about community. Instead of control, it is about trust. Precisely those who are excluded by the system are in the centre of it. Those who rule will have to learn to wash the feet of others. The poor are first in line: the lepers, the children, but equally so the tax-collector or the fortune-seeking refugee who is ignored by the crowd.

The kingdom of which Jesus speaks in the four gospels is not some spiritual ideal which will only be realized in heaven. According to the authors of the Bible, it is a kingdom that will cover both heaven and earth. The word "kingdom" bears a political connotation, "kingdom" being similar to "empire" in the Roman Empire. Like "savior" and "gospel" it's a political word which was used by the Romans to tell the world that peace and prosperity came on earth by the grace of the emperor and his legions. This new kingdom, however, is diametrically opposed to the "empire of the world", which is ruled by powers and systems who think they are gods but in reality are very weak.

Obviously, this is a story that directly challenges the elite. Jesus with his kingdom does not fit within the empire of the world. The steps Jesus takes on the ladder of success are actually downwards. As he walks towards the center of religious and worldly power, he leaves behind everything he has. The path Jesus follows is one of letting go of all means to power and status. The only instrument he has is a group of fallible men and women who are his friends. In a world that only thinks in terms of effect, means, and power, Jesus chooses powerlessness and friendship. This is revolutionary, because by doing so he undermines the divinity of the prevailing order, of both the religious and political elites. Hence it is not a surprise that both elites together decide there is only one way to stop this: execution.

* * *

Girard, the social scientist, was impressed by this story, just when he was formulating his famous theory that explained how religion is always based on mimetic violence and the sacrifice of the scapegoat. Right through to the end Jesus is not lead by worldly desires, and he denies every form of mimetic rivalry. When you follow him it is impossible to become his rival, Girard says, because he steps aside. Jesus does not compete with anyone, and willingly takes on the role of scapegoat, a position of shame and exclusion. Through to the end Jesus withstands the power of the powers that be, with their idea about ends justifying means. Without resistance he lets himself be crucified, not out of weakness, but because his authority is one that is stronger than the survival of the fittest. Jesus is so free that he does not even hold on to his own life.

We know of the curious consequence: a movement of people comes into existence who say he has risen from the dead. In fact: that he came from God, that he was God himself. Now, there are scores of myths about godlike men who were killed and rose again, but none of them believed in a god that laid down his life voluntarily, without using violence. The story spread like wildfire throughout the entire Roman Empire, because people believed this was about more than a singular miracle. One miracle would never have motivated them to be eaten alive by lions in the Colosseum. They truly believed that the mechanism of rivalry and exclusion did not have the final say anymore, not even death, and that it is possible to escape the laws of causality if we stop holding on to the means and powers that we invoke time and again because we are afraid to lose what we have. In other words, they started to believe there was a power, righteous and just, that was stronger than the worldly powers.

Does one have to believe this if one wants to be able to live differently? I don't think so; you can also live differently without believing it. But a second question is more interesting: is it necessary for the above to have really happened to free the world from the powers that threaten us? In other words: where do we find an authority that can truly liberate us from our imprisonment? It is up to each one of us to figure out an answer to this question, to search in earnest where to find real hope. I have chosen to put my faith in this bizarre story.

That is what someone like Ellul did as well. At an age of twenty he had a deep spiritual experience. It gave him enough faith to declare for the rest of his life that there is a power and a justice outside our human systems. And this in turn helped him not to descend into depression due to his own severe analyses.

You might say that Ellul always looked at the world through two pairs of glasses.[2] One pair, borrowed from Marx, showed him the material facts of poverty, unemployment, estrangement: the powers that threaten our world with destruction. The other pair came from his Christian faith. Ellul posits that God does not fit within a religion or an ethical framework. To declare that he does so would be an attempt to once again force freedom into a system. Not religion, but *faith* is the opposite of technique. Faith is a matter of love, a reply to God's love: that is freedom. At the same time, through this radical faith-based freedom, we can position ourselves in those systems differently.

Ellul's two pairs of glasses enabled him to look evil in the eye in earnest, without adding a juicy optimistic sauce in order not to make people despair. He calls this dialectical thinking, giving new meaning to an old term used by Hegel and Marx. Some contradictions cannot be resolved by theorizing about them, Ellul says, but only by living them. It is no coincidence that the first disciples of Jesus were not called the people of the doctrine or the people of the new philosophy, but the "people of the way".

In short, living spiritually means more than simply meditating and always having a smile on your face. It means living from the belief in a new, deeper reality, in a life we cannot make, manipulate, or control, but that is given us from above. Then we will also be bestowed with an identity that is not dependent on what

2. As Ellul himself explained in *Perspectives on Our Age*.

others think of us and which enables us to ignore the voices of fear. The next chapter will deal with how to put this into practice.

11

Back to Reality

*How the good life is found in stubborn reality,
in poor neighborhoods and dirty gardens,
in the middle of the tears and joy of life
in community.*

THE DILAPIDATED GARAGE DOORS behind our house are as charming as a Belarusian parking lot. The doors are kept together with makeshift latches, under balconies from which the paint comes peeling off. The square in front of the house is surrounded by gray four-story building blocks for which no one has cared at least the last thirty years. A Turkish-looking woman with a headscarf is doing her laundry, as usual, and her neighbor is shouting to his child downstairs in the Moroccan Berber language. As usual. Two boys on their scooters are racing up and down the street, without helmets, practicing a wheelie.

On one of the sides of the square there's a former shopping block with upstairs apartments. In front of this building, under a few sycamore trees struggling to survive in this stony desert, we ·

have prepared a dinner for a group consisting of a colorful mixture of people, and when Iranian and Syrian food is served I feel proud to say that this is my home.

I live in this community which I started with a few friends in 2008. I was just married when we got the chance to rent a few apartments in an empty block that was destined to be demolished. We decided this was the most ugly place in town, in a neighborhood that was number one on all the wrong lists. We lived together, ate together, set some rooms apart for refugees, had dinners with neighbors, had weekly prayers and organized game and movie nights with neighbors and friends. At times we have been completely fed up with everything, but at the same time we have learned to love this place.

I want to tell you something about this, not to explain how I think you should live as an ethically good citizen, but because this book is about the good life, the real life, and this real life is not found in a theory but in life itself: on squares, in dilapidated buildings and under sycamore trees. In many other places, too, obviously, but I want to give the example of my own life to make clear what I mean when I write about focusing on the way or the means, instead of the results or the ends. It's a plea for real life, for stubborn reality with all of its limitations, because that—rather than the shining lie of hyperreality—is where the good life can be found.

* * *

The good life is not the same as the successful life, not even when you define success as, for example, finding solutions to world problems. If I focus on the here and now, other things emerge as important goals of the day. Sometimes just working hard, for example, to earn my living. But sometimes reading a book with my son about dinosaurs. Sometimes taking care of the apple tree we planted behind our house, sometimes taking time to learn to play a new song on my ukulele. Sometimes giving my money to someone who is in debt, or a room to a guest, or not seeing anyone because it's time for rest, or for romance or music. Putting energy, in short, into things that are inherently good, that would also have value if the Earth were to perish next year. For me there is a very simple way to find out what is hyper and not hyper in our rich and affluent society: ask yourself if what you do is a goal in itself, if it is the good life in itself. The good life is not the same as the feelgood life.

Living like this doesn't leave much time for collecting stuff. Not that "stuff" is necessarily bad. Money, a car, a career, a position, things, Facebook friends, status, media: all of these are not necessarily "bad" per se, but they tend to trap you by becoming indispensable. The best litmus test I can apply to check if they have become powers that rule over my life is to do what powers usually don't like: sharing. I can share money by dropping it in someone's post box anonymously. Or by doing voluntary work. Not just to achieve something, but because it is healthy and liberating to share. I can also share control. I can try to empower others, I can train myself to listen to other people in a group where many people tend to listen to me. I can also share status, by opening my life for people without status. For people who are not so cool, who are not so dynamic, or even have no legal right to live in my country. If I do that, I use the means available without giving them any power.

* * *

One way that helps me to share, to share my life, is to do it collectively, in the neighborhood I have described. In our society we often have too much space for ourselves, too many walls, big fenced-off gardens and too many things. Living together with others is a way to share this. We have an apartment of our own, my wife and four kids, but we share our lives and our building with a bigger community, so I am constantly unlearning my exaggerated need for privacy. When we look back over the last twelve years we feel that in a certain way that this is really healthy for us.

We call ourselves Overhoop, which is a combination of Overvecht (the name of the neighborhood) and hope, but in Dutch it also means something like messy, upside-down. For us, this living together is something spiritual. That does not only mean praying or singing together, but also sharing a washing machine or giving a room to a refugee or to someone who is just divorced. And also having a second-hand shop where everything is free, and where you can find the strangest people on Earth. Or organizing community action against government plans to sell our square to a property developer (a struggle we have recently won because we have more friends in town than the developer).

We have formed a church together with others in the neighborhood. "Church" might sound very religious for some, and we do follow Jesus, but for us this heavy-laden term just means coming together with people from different social and ethnic backgrounds for prayer and meals, and caring for each other, in other words: being a family.

Often it costs a lot of energy, sometimes too much. But at the same time it makes us very, very rich. We have more frustrations and tears than we did before, but also more music, cake, parties and deep friendships with people from all over the world. Sometimes I lie awake, full of sorrow about some of our friends who cannot escape their traumas and depressions, who feel bad and sometimes even turn against us because they find it almost unbearable to trust someone. But at other times I find myself dancing to Kurdish music in our community living room because someone just got his residence permit after nine years of waiting. We have exchanged a piece of hyperreality for the deep reality: the good life with God and other people.

Many people I meet call this "idealistic", but it is not. On the contrary, we have discovered idealism to be a trap. If we let ourselves be guided by ideals, we start to aim for a certain perfection we will never be able to reach. Those are goals which steer my thinking automatically towards more resources and influence, without addressing my self-centeredness and they usually result in judging other people. There are always housemates or other people who don't fit into whatever nice plan I might have come up with.

Ideals should never take precedence, but rather the Way, the good life, should take the lead. The way is a rocky path ("The road to hell is paved with good intentions, the road to heaven is not paved," is what the American traveler music group the Psalters shouted once, when they performed in our house). The good way is bumpy. Sometimes we ask ourselves what on earth we are doing after wasting our time on a useless house meeting about how to interpret a certain rule. Or we organize something that attracts only white people and we feel that we have failed in our good intentions. Many more times we are hurt by someone, often by someone we took in for a few months and who left without saying thank you or goodbye. The well-known priest Henri Nouwen writes about the difference between effect and fruit.[1] We shouldn't worry about effect, he says; we should live in order to bear fruit. Sometimes our plans fail. Sometimes groups fall apart. Or people die. But we are not responsible for the amount of fruit we generate, only for the Way we follow.

* * *

The British doctor Paul Brand, who died in 2003, worked his whole life with lepers in India, Ethiopia and the US. During his research he made a revolutionary discovery. Apparently, the deformations to the leper's body were not the result of the disease itself, as had always been thought. Limbs hurt and died off because people wounded themselves by accident, because they couldn't feel pain. Leprosy doesn't kill the limbs, but the nervous system, he discovered. Brand wrote a book about it, *Pain: The Gift that Nobody Wants*. Healing a leper means giving him back his pain.[2]

We, the children of hyperreality, have a kind of leprosy, too. We don't have a connection anymore to the pain of real life. Pain is bad, we think, and should be abolished, by pills or by concentrating it in a home for the elderly at a safe distance from society. As a result we are numbed and this is what kills us slowly. To be healed we must open ourselves to the pain again. To be able to see the stars, we first have to turn off the lights.

Living in a community in a poor neighborhood helps me to be healed from the leprosy of hyperreality. It helps me to wake up

1. For example in his books *Here and Now*, and *The Road to Peace*.
2. Brand, *Pain*.

from the "Suburban Lifestyle Dream", as a former US President called this, where one is not "bothered by low income housing".[3] We are bothered indeed. We are bothered by broken families and children who shout or even fight on the street. We are bothered by broken people who become my friends but still bear the scars of trauma, alcohol and personality disorders. My happiness is bothered when one of my friends is taken to a detention center because the authorities don't want him in my country. I am bothered when my housemate can't sleep because he misses his children in Eritrea whom he hasn't seen for three years.

This shatters my shiny Suburban Lifestyle Dream into pieces and warps me back into reality in a split second. But unexpectedly it gives me more reason to get out of bed in the morning. It gives me reasons to fight. It's healthy to learn to struggle and fight, in a society where we are so amused that we are bored to death.

It liberates me from a lot of illusions. When boys on the street smash my door, the illusion that I am a quite decent guy is smashed with it, since I feel an anger coming up from deep within and I discover myself to be able to sentence a whole ethnic group to a re-education camp in my mind. This part of me would not be uncovered if I stayed in the city center, working behind my laptop with my latte macchiato and a brownie.

More illusions die here. Our faith in the human ability to re-make the world, for example. If I sometimes imagine the amount of sadness around our square, the depressions, the fights, the debts, the joblessness, and other worries. . . it seems so desperate, there is absolutely no way that the state or social institutions will ever solve these problems. The only thing we hope and pray for is: God, have mercy.

And unexpectedly, sometimes indeed things happen which are too miraculous to describe. In the midst of this stubborn and painful reality we discover glimpses of a reality that is fuller and richer that I often dare to believe in. If people start to dare to give themselves, if they start to care for each other, if we unexpectedly get the impossible chance to buy our house and even find the

3. Trump, Twitter Post.

money for it, if we look around the table and see all these strange people mixed together and someone grabs an accordion and makes everyone dance, including Samira, the Somali headscarved woman who has never danced before, at these moments I wonder if miracles do exist. Sometimes hopeless people feel enabled to change their lives because they have seen something from God. This all gives a depth that I can't find in hyperreality.

Again, it is not true that poor people are better people. I encounter many people here who are difficult to deal with. Life here is not healthy. Life in the city is not healthy: I have a strong feeling deep within that we are not made for it. But the encounter with poverty, with brokenness, with community, is healthy since it connects me to the pain of the world, it rescues me from the trance of hyperreality and it gives me more joy than I could even find in the Suburban Lifestyle Dream. Let's not forget this word, *joy*. It's not the same as being happy. It's fresh and life-giving.

It's not only community between rich and poor that can save us from hyperreality. Some people find it in music or literature or other forms of art. Or in nature, in wilderness, where life is not over-clean and optimized and where we can be touched by an impressive creativity which is freely available, which takes its time, and which doesn't impose itself.

This is the reason that I share a small vegetable garden with some friends, just five minutes away. I know that the philosophers and technicians may find in this a proof of my romanticism. But it helps me to connect to the ground. I don't just feel the earth, but also the sun and the rain and my body. It gives me muscle pain and hunger, which I can still with an apple that I picked myself. It's as if I activate parts of my body that I lost connection with.

Nature is not a luxury, it's a pure necessity. I think of this when I look at the Turkish and Moroccan and other boys in my neighborhood, trapped in their own hyperreality of concrete, scooters, violent movies and money, while at the same time trying to look like a pious Muslim on the outside. In a certain way their life is detached from reality, too. With a few of them I have quite a good connection, but it's easier to pierce their armor when you take them out of their habitat. For that reason I once took them to a very small forest, in the middle of the night, to make a little campfire on the top of an old bunker, fry some halal sausages and teach them fire breathing. It's only seven minutes by bicycle, but they had never been there. They were scared in the dark, these macho men, but they experienced a little bit of this joy. One of them even said thank you afterwards.

* * *

A very simple way to break the connection with hyperreality for a while is an old trick: stop eating for a day. It's not for nothing that fasting is a very important element of so many spiritual traditions. If I don't eat for a day, consciously, I feel how much my whole life turns around comfort and feeling nice, if only through coffee and snacks. Skipping that is not cool, it's not comfortable and it even makes me a bit sad. But it is a really simple method to step out of the permanent Jacuzzi around me, to say no to the siren song of everything that promises me contentment.

You can also take a fast from incentives. To be someone, to become someone, we need that: spaces where there are no others, no opinions, no news. We need free space in our life, space where we're not distracted and influenced. We don't have to know all the latest news. We don't have to be online all the time. People often wonder how I can be a journalist without a television and without a smartphone because they think it necessary in order to be connected to the world. For me it's the other way around. I didn't become a journalist to help grow the information mountain, I became a journalist to help people think. Thinking becomes much easier when you pull the plug from the media and start to talk to people, read books and be silent. Not knowing the latest remark made by whatever politician or expert is not a high price to pay.

"Instead of thought there is a vast, inhuman void, full of words, formulas, slogans, declarations, echoes, ideologies," wrote the famous writer-monk Thomas Merton. According to him our thinking is numbed by media we passively swallow. We need silence in order to think. We need contemplation.

III: DAZZLING FREEDOM

If we do not think, we cannot act freely; we are at the mercy of forces, which we never understand, forces that are arbitrary, destructive, blind, fatal to us and our world.[4]

Merton himself was a very political writer. His articles about the nuclear arms race and the Vietnam War were very widely read and they are still a source of wisdom for anyone who wants to understand the psychology of war. Yet it took several weeks before the outcome of the presidential election in the US reached him.

If we become silent, we step out of the hectic tangle of mimetic relationships. We need solitude sometimes. Without others we don't have a community, or an identity, but sometimes we need to step back and stand still to contemplate our relationships to other people. And to God, who is most of the time a silent God, a God who doesn't shout but whisper, a whisper we can't hear until we silence all other sounds. Ultimately that's where we can find an identity that gives rest, an identity that you can't prove or defend. That is a force that can beat the deep fear that we all have inside of us, a force that can also beat the need to control our lives. Only then we can become really free. I admit that I am not good at it, being silent. Sometimes I long for silence, but with a lot of thoughts in my head, email in my inbox, and children in my room, it's hard to find it. I sincerely wonder how friends with a smartphone ever manage to find it.

* * *

My spiritual worldview is not just just a private matter, though. I think spiritual living can help us to make better political choices. Based on what we have discovered about ends and means we could formulate an ethical framework for politicians and policy makers. Instead of measures that provide us with more means, which we trust, which we load with symbolic value, which increase our power in the hope that it pays off later, we should use as a criterion that a measure in itself should be good. Economic growth, becoming the

4. Merton, *Conjectures*, 74.

largest agricultural exporter, liberalizing the labor market, tapping internet conversations, bombing the enemy: before anything we should ask ourselves: what are the real consequences, what does it really give us, is this measure really good and valuable *in itself*?

Sometimes leaders are able to do this. An example for me is the nuclear disarmament at the end of the Cold War. Ronald Reagan and Mikhail Gorbachev were, by the end of the eighties, ready and willing to reduce their nuclear stockpile because they dared to question the consequences of continuing the arms race. This rational attitude became possible because of two things: firstly, because of the economic burnout of one party, the Soviet Union; but secondly because of the moral turnaround they had each separately experienced. They had the courage and the faith, to the horror of their generals and their foreign policy advisers, to trust their own convictions and also the other's. They decided to dismantle thousands of nuclear warheads. It is an historic example of leaders who consciously decided to step out of the mimetic rivalry that held both societies in their evil grip.

The leaders themselves had wanted even more, but unfortunately the system was too strong for that. At this very moment the US still have around 5000 warheads, Russia around 4000. It is clear that a change of course cannot easily come from the top. That was what Ellul has also discovered, to his great disappointment, when he served as a deputy mayor in Bordeaux for a while, just after the war. Politics has become an instrument of the technological system, he concluded. A change is only possible with a deep, moral turnaround, together with structural changes. But the system is strong. He wrote:

> The only successful way to attack these features of modern civilization is to give them the slip, to learn how to live on the edge of this totalitarian society, not simply rejecting it, but passing it through the sieve of God's judgment. Finally, when communities with a "style of life" of this kind have been established, possibly the first signs of a new civilization may begin to appear.[5]

5. Ellul, *Presence*, 46.

That is an active spirituality. Already, in the thirties, Ellul, together with his friend Bernard Charbonneau, founded youth groups to draw young people away from the propaganda from the totalitarian left and right. He took students into the mountains, for weeks, as a kind of a parallel university outside the civilized world. There they could debate and think about society, study difficult writers like Tocqueville or Kierkegaard, and at the same time learn to bake their own bread in a self-built oven.

Ellul doesn't call on us to retreat into the mountains, without smartphone and microwave, to return to a kind of happy, atechnological state of mind with self-baked bread. He didn't believe in that. His hope for us was to find our freedom again by becoming subjects, humans enabled to think and judge for ourselves, in the midst of a technical-economic system reducing us to cogs in the machine. Of course we are conditioned from top to toe. We must start by acknowledging this, because then we judge it, and in moral judgment lies our freedom. Let's use this dazzling freedom, Ellul proclaimed at the end of his life, to fill the cracks that will surely appear in society when the machine pushes up against its boundaries.

That's a mission I want to join in wholeheartedly. Cracks will appear: they appear all the time. Dark clouds are coming. Resources run dry, communities are undermined and mimetic rivalry is howling through the streets and the dark alleys of social media. Resentment and victim thinking tempts groups to see others as a dangerous enemy. Not only in the West, but also in many poorer countries, where leaders are kept in place because we need their resources and cheap labor to keep our machine going.

Let's start acknowledging this. Only then we can actively start to search for signs of hope. Let's use our technologically-conditioned eyes to find signs of life outside our human systems. That's no escapism: that is an active attitude that can sow the seed of something new.

Epilogue: Theology and Hope

How this story translates in theological terms, and why we need apocalyptic thinking.

Another world is not only possible, she is on her way. On a quiet day, I can hear her breathing.

<small>ARUNDHATI ROY[1]</small>

WHERE ARE WE HEADING? The monsters we have created are so strong and so deadly that we often look away and try to forget they exist, so as not to be caught by pessimism or even despair. Yet for us, if we want to live a meaningful life, if we want to find the good life in the midst of this broken and painful reality, it's crucial to face this despair and to find a way through it. To me, the Christian faith offers a healthy way of doing that. I don't like to force people to swallow a Christian message, but my faith does shape my ideas about everything we've talked about. That is why I want to spend a few words on it in this epilogue.

At first glance, Christianity doesn't always offer a convincing answer to hyperreality. Church speak and evangelical metaphors

---

1. Roy, *Ordinary Person's Guide to Empire*, 86.

have taken on a life of their own, and often don't really connect to the reality of people spiralling into burnouts, divorce or just boredom, let alone to the reality of the ongoing destruction of nature. Much of our spiritual discourse neglects the trap we have fallen into, the trap of our desires, our systems, and the inevitable price we will have to pay for that.

In other words, Christianity, too, has become hyperreal. And just as hyperreality is a projection of our desires, the Christian message and the shape it takes in many churches has been molded and adapted to their members' desires. Faith should make us happy. It should solve our private problems, it should be fun, the music performed in church should be professional and the plasma screens huge. Its community should be cool and have real influence in the world. And if this community no longer meets our expectations, if the people are too conservative, the pastor too left-wing or the coffee too strong, we just head on to the next one. Or we stop belonging to communities at all. After all, we are so incredibly busy, we'd rather skip some things!

* * *

I believe the real story of the Bible is one of liberation. How we can be liberated from forces (including death) that hold us captive, enslave us, keep us weak and alone. Seen from a human perspective, we are trapped. We so desperately want a beautiful world, yet we have to acknowledge that uncontrollable powers force us into the opposite direction.[2]

---

2. A beautiful book about this is Shane Claiborne and Chris Haw's *Jesus for President*, though they might give the impression that the apocalypse is "only" a warning. Also important is Walter Wink's trilogy, *The Powers That Be*, of which a compilation appeared in 1998. He was one of the first to develop a theology of the powers. Except for Ellul, who had already written a lot on this theme, for example in his Bible study *The Meaning of the City* and his related study about the Book of Revelation, *Apocalypse: The Book of Revelations*. For me the books of N.T. Wright are also helpful in discovering what was actually at the core of the gospel story, for example *How God Became King: The Forgotten Story of the Gospels*.

EPILOGUE: THEOLOGY AND HOPE

Our fight is not against humans of flesh and blood, the apostle Paul writes in his letters, but against the spiritual powers and governments that rule the world. Paul does not mean dark spirits smelling of sulphur. He talks of the powers we have discussed above, the powers that blind us and make us forget what our existence is meant for. These can become demonic.

The powers have a hold on a weak part of us that Paul calls the flesh. This word, flesh, is often associated with sex, but in the Bible, it refers to any desire that is aimed towards something that can't fulfill us. "Sin" literally means "missing the mark". In the end, the worship of those powers is worship of ourselves. We believe in our tools because we believe we can control them. We believe we understand the difference between good and evil. It's hubris mixed with fear: fear of running short, fear of losing.

Theologian Jürgen Moltmann writes how our unquenchable thirst for life ultimately comes from a fear of death. Note how he mentions the same three promises of hyperreality we talked about.

> This fear of death finds expression in an unbridled hunger for power. "You only live once!" we are told. "You might miss out on something!" This hunger for pleasure, for possessions, for power; the thirst for recognition through success and admiration; that is the perversion of modern men and women. That is their godlessness. The person who loses God makes a god out of himself. And in this way a human being becomes a proud and unhappy mini-god.[3]

* * *

The Bible tells of the path God wanted to walk with us. The Hebrew law was designed for a different way, for a society characterized by peace, harmony, and wholeness. Many of the Old Testament prescriptions are meant to limit the destructive mechanisms we have discussed earlier. The year of Jubilee, for example, in which everyone's debts are canceled, every fifty years. Or the stipulation

---

3. Moltmann, *Source*, 107.

about gleaning: the Israelites had to leave the edges of their fields during harvest in order to always leave something for the poor and the foreigner. There is nothing wrong with trade and markets, as long as there is a gray zone left for the outsiders. The story of Ruth from Moab (an illegal immigrant, since Israel was a no-go area for Moabites) shows that even for unwanted people, systems should never be entirely closed.

It is important to note that the Torah doesn't deny our human needs. We cannot live without material security, safety, and a community to which we belong. We do not have to change this. We are allowed to seek fulfilment of our needs. And if we do this the right way, by not turning to exploitation of the poor, to idols who demand human sacrifices or to world powers who seduce us with their chariots or their missiles, but by "acting justly, loving mercy and walking humbly with your God" (Micah 6:8) we will see our land flourish with grain, peace, and harmony. In fact, we are promised a deep satisfaction of all of our needs, deeper than we might even dare to desire.

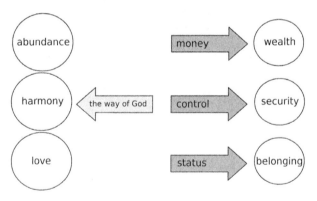

The Torah promises us things greater than our desires

Our needs are not bad. Yet our desires are aimed in the wrong direction, as are as the means we use to achieve them. We are eager to fulfil our desires with fake surrogates. Note that our desires are watered-down reflections of the abundance we are offered. As C.S. Lewis famously put it:

It would seem that Our Lord finds our desires not too
strong, but too weak. We are half-hearted creatures, fool-
ing about with drink and sex and ambition when infinite
joy is offered us, like an ignorant child who wants to go
on making mud pies in a slum because he cannot imagine what is meant by the offer of a holiday at the sea. We
are far too easily pleased.[4]

If we put our trust in the wrong means and powers, then we
will not find peace and harmony, or *shalom*, the prophets warned,
but the judgement of God. That might sound harsh, but for them
this "judgment" is the logical consequence of our actions, inseparable from the bad systems we believe in. Eventually, all these powers and systems will turn against us. In fact, what you worship is
what you will look like, one of the Psalmists writes. This is how
God created the world, we might say; hence God "punishes" much
as God draws an apple to the ground if you open your hand. That
is how the law of cause and effect works: like karma.

I think there is more truth to this than we are willing to admit
nowadays. In hyperreality, we try to undo the laws of cause and
consequence; indeed, of judgment. But in the end we will not be
able to escape it, and that judgment will come upon us—whether
in the shape of depleted oceans, terrorism, or depression.

* * *

Karma is fair. But God's ways are higher than karma. According
to the authors of the Bible, God loves us. He wants to set us free
from karma and from the powers. The prophets told Israel time
and again that God would send a special man who would do just
that. A righteous king who would not only give us just laws but
even a new heart; a king who would give us real peace and take the
judgment, however deserved, from us.

And then something unbelievable enters the story. Suddenly,
the Jewish writers start to claim that this godly king has arrived in
the form of a simple man called Jesus. He lived as God intended
and chose the radical path in direct opposition to the powers. He

4. Lewis, *Weight of Glory*, 26.

129

did not listen to the laws of the city ot to his own fear of death. He wandered around and brought people together from all social classes. It cost him his life, as they executed him in a mock coronation ritual.

So did he lose? Did the powers have the final say after all? According to Ellul, there is something that escapes the logic of cause and consequence. It is God. Life itself. According to the gospel writers, God himself intervened and changed the course of history by resurrecting this man from the dead: Jesus, the humble king that did not bow to the powers. All this to prove—the writers say with disbelief, amazement, joy—that this king will be the one to judge us, that he is maybe God himself, that there is more than karma, more than our destructive tendencies, and more than our fatal human systems.

This news is actually too bizarre to simply discuss in a book about money, power, and technique. In fact, it is less believable than a fairy tale. But imagine. Imagine if this unthinkable story were actually true. Imagine that someone was able to oppose the worldly powers without giving in. And that even death itself. . . then maybe he really is . . . then maybe there is hope . . . then, at the heart of the lion's den, of the powers that rage around the world and cast her into violence, exhaustion and poverty, a bridgehead has been built to the Other side, by the God who created life from death before, and who apparently likes us so much that he wants to do it again for us.

I have to admit that this is the only story that is able to give me goose bumps if I let it get to me. It is the only story that offers me a sometimes incomprehensible but nevertheless jaw-dropping answer to the destruction our society is heading towards. And that is why I hold on to it. Other writers I have mentioned have come to realize the same. Lewis, for example, and Ellul, Merton, Girard, Dostoevsky: all of them discovered this secret at a certain point in their lives and decided that this secret was what they wanted to live for.[5] They believed our world is in crisis, a spiritual crisis, from which only the God of resurrection can save us.

5. Also, writer Paul Kingsnorth, who helped me translate this book,

EPILOGUE: THEOLOGY AND HOPE

* * *

Listening to Christian people around me, I see two major pitfalls. The first is mixing faith with the agenda of progress. Trying to build God's kingdom ourselves, right here on earth, by making everybody equal and happy, either through the church or the state or through medical science. It will lead to nothing, like any other movement in history that attempted to build God's kingdom on earth led to nothing—at best. It directs our attention towards social changes, but it forgets that the reality of evil powers is not something that can be broken by a political program.

The second pitfall believers tumble into is the opposite one: spiritualizing the kingdom of God. Heaven is our home, they say, not earth. Is not the salvation of our soul the end goal? Especially in America, whole school classes sign contracts with their parents that they will save sex for marriage, but see no problem in supporting presidents or oil companies that exploit the earth for money. Everything will perish in fire, after all. This form of Christianity, too, forgets the reality of our slavery, and believes we can escape it by adhering to some secret code (for example, a certain theory about the subsidiary punishment of Jesus). Essentially this is the old pitfall of Gnosticism. Gnostics believed the physical was less valuable than the spiritual; that in order to escape the physical and enter God's kingdom we should become aware of secret insights and that way we will be saved from the earthly problems.

Jesus and his followers taught something else. Firstly, they didn't talk about anything like a separation between body and soul. As Jews, they regarded these as interwoven. Secondly, they didn't tell us that a certain knowledge would liberate us, but only love, and faith—in a Person, not in beliefs. Knowledge does not exist in a pure, objective form, separate from people. Postmodern thinkers have figured this out recently. The authors of the Bible already knew it. Knowledge is preceded and defined by relations, by love

---

recently wrote me he felt unable to resist this secret any longer, much to his own surprise. Read his essays to learn more, since he writes much better than me.

and by power. Hence it can only be learned through relations, in reality, and passed on by relations, through time.

When the Bible talks about heaven, it is not referring to some thin, serene dimension, with floating angels on weightless clouds, where we eat easily digestible porridge with golden spoons eternally. Heaven as a geographical place is a metaphor by the biblical writers to indicate the presence of God. Heaven does not relate to earth, writes Lewis, as a shadow does to a vase, but rather as a flower does to a seed. It is not some kind of virtual reality without time and the laws of nature, but a tangible world in which the curtain between heaven and earth will have been lifted. It is a "kingdom" in the Bible, a tangible reality in the future, so true and tangible that our current reality will appear a faint alternative.

This gospel is "good news" indeed, since in our times, the powers seem to be more dangerous than ever. The technical system is expanding and is colonising an ever growing part of our lives. Simultaneously, the reaction of people who feel rejected all over the world is becoming more passionate and violent. Dark clouds are gathering. I have to admit I often miss a sense of urgency around me in the well-off part of the world, even in church. What we dearly lack is an apocalyptic awareness. Yes, I mean apocalypse, as referred to in the book of Revelation; a book which was never meant as a storyboard, by the way, but as a dramatic (and prophetic) glimpse of the dynamic of powers increasingly turning to violence. This is not an apocalypse in the popular sense, as in the radical Islamic or American evangelical visions of Christ coming back to annihilate Earth. To the contrary, with humankind seemingly ready to annihilate Earth, or at least to cling to the powers who are ready to destroy, it's Christ who inspires us to peer through the cracks and to discern what's really true and just and lasting.

Apocalyptic expectation, in this sense, is about a future which comes to us irrevocably, which breaks into our iron systems and changes our reality, not without us, but by waking us up and empowering us to resist, in the midst of violence. Much as the landing in Normandy fundamentally turned around all authority and power relations in the occupied territories. This did not mean that the occupation was over. On the contrary, it became all the more bloody, and it took a winter before D-Day was followed by the final victory over the Nazis. But the real decision was made on D-Day, when the victorious future broke into the reality of the war and changed the minds of the people.

Apocalyptic thinking in this sense means that we continuously discern two movements: evil is growing, but goodness, too. It means that we can appreciate science and justice and social order, but simultaneously acknowledge that our rationality has become so powerful we can destroy the whole world with it. The powers are greater than ever, yet also weaker than ever. Left to themselves they hold little persuasive authority, but still they are able to amass a lot of oppressive power, and many people find themselves at loss how to deal with them.

People find it difficult to face both sides honestly, Ellul said. They believe in either/or, or they sugarcoat their pessimistic fears with politically correct optimism. Ellul makes the case for thinking dialectically, as we have discussed before. Sociologically we should acknowledge—as Marxists do—that structural powers are enslaving us. But with spiritual eyes we can see—in opposition to Marxists—that God is acting in history, that He made Christ king over all the powers, even money and missiles, even death itself. We have to think through both opposites, according to Ellul. The tension between them cannot be resolved in theory. You can only live it in practice, by letting yourself be changed by this future.

Death is undoing itself like a woollen sweater hooked on a nail. How God will save us, I wouldn't dare to predict. Whether it happens gradually or rapidly, what the kingdom of God really means, and what our roles within it will be, I do not know. What I do believe is that we need this apocalyptic perspective. The technical system is subjugating earth, more limitless than ever. There is much more at stake than we sometimes realize. I think we are preparing for a great destruction.

III: DAZZLING FREEDOM

But D-Day is behind us. There has been an invasion from the Other side, and the bridgehead is holding on. There might be a dark winter ahead, but liberation is inevitable.

* * *

The future is not hyper at all. It is physical and real, more real and tangible than our current reality. It is described beautifully in Isaiah's vision about what is in the mind of the Eternal, the creator of all powers we have discussed. He invites us to a meal with all peoples together, where wine is plenty and the false promises come undone for once and for all. This is an apocalyptic perspective that puts everything we do today in a completely different light. This celebration is what we are moving towards. It is up to us to prepare for this celebration in the reality of our everyday lives.

> On this mountain the Lord Almighty will prepare
> a feast of rich food for all peoples,
> a banquet of aged wine—
> the best of meats and the finest of wines.
> On this mountain he will destroy
> the shroud that enfolds all peoples,
> the sheet that covers all nations;
> he will swallow up death forever.
> The Sovereign Lord will wipe away the tears
> from all faces;
> he will remove his people's disgrace
> from all the earth.
> The Lord has spoken.[6]

6. Isa 25:6–8.

Bibliography

Arendt, Hannah. *Eichmann in Jerusalem: A Report on the Banality of Evil.* New York: Penguin, 2006.

Baudrillard, Jean. *Simulacres et Simulation.* Paris: Galilée, 1981.

Carr, Nicholas. *The Glass Cage: How Our Computers Are Changing Us.* New York: W. W. Norton & Company, 2015.

————. *The Shallows: What the Internet is Doing to Our Brains.* New York: W.W. Norton, 2011.

Claiborne, Shane, and Chris Haw. *Jesus For President: Politics for Ordinary Radicals.* Grand Rapids, Mich: Zondervan, 2008.

Dostoyevsky, Fyodor, Richard Pevear, and Larissa Volokhonsky. *The Brothers Karamazov.* New York: Knopf Distributed by Random House, 1992.

Eco, Umberto. *Travels in Hyperreality: essays.* San Diego: Harcourt Brace Jovanovich, 1990.

Ellsberg, Daniel. *The Doomsday Machine: Confessions of a Nuclear War Planner.* New York: Bloomsbury, 2017.

Ellul, Jacques. *Apocalypse: The Book of Revelation.* New York: Seabury, 1977.

————. *The Presence of the Kingdom.* Colorado Springs: Helmers & Howard, 1989.

————. *The Technological Society.* New York: Vintage, 1964.

Ellul, Jacques, and Joyce M. Hanks. *The Humiliation of the Word.* Grand Rapids, Michigan: Eerdmans, 1985.

Ellul, Jacques, and Willem H. Vanderburg. *Perspectives on Our Age: Jacques Ellul Speaks on His Life and Work.* Toronto: House of Anansi, 1997.

Gandhi, and Valji G. Desai. *Satyagraha in South Africa.* Ahmedabad: Navajivan, 1997.

Girard, René. *Things Hidden Since the Foundation of the World.* Stanford, Calif: Stanford University Press, 1987.

Goudzwaard, B., Mark V. Vennen, and David Heemst. *Hope in Troubled Times: a New Vision for Confronting Global Crises.* Grand Rapids, Mich: Baker Academic, 2007.

Holland, Tom. *Dominion: How the Christian Revolution Remade the World.* New York: Basic, 2019.

Huxley, Aldous. *Brave New World.* New York: Perennial Classics, 1998.

———. *Ends and Means: An Inquiry Into the Nature of Ideals.* New Brunswick, N.J: Transaction, 2012.

Kelly, Kevin. *What Technology Wants.* New York: Viking, 2010.

Kingsnorth, Paul. *Confessions of a Recovering Environmentalist and Other Essays.* Minneapolis, MN: Graywolf, 2017.

Lewis, C. S. *The Abolition of Man, or, Reflections on Education With Special Reference to the Teaching of English in the Upper Forms of Schools.* San Francisco: HarperSanFrancisco, 2001.

Lewis, C. S., and Walter Hooper. *The Weight of Glory and Other Addresses.* San Francisco: HarperSanFrancisco, 2001.

Luyendijk, Joris. *Among the Bankers: A Journey into the Heart of Finance.* Brooklyn: Melville House, 2016.

Moltmann, Jürgen. *The Source of Life: The Holy Spirit and the Theology of Life.* Minneapolis: Fortress, 1997.

Morozov, Evgeny. *The Net Delusion: The Dark Side of Internet Freedom.* New York: Public Affairs, 2011.

——— *To Save Everything, Click Here: The Folly of Technological Solutionism.* New York: PublicAffairs, 2013.

Nouwen, Henri J. *Here and Now: Living in the Spirit.* New York: Crossroad, 2006.

Nouwen, Henri J., and John Dear. *The Road to Peace: Writings on Peace and Justice.* Maryknoll, N.Y: Orbis, 2003.

Ortega y Gasset, Jose, *The Revolt of the Masses.* New York: W.W. Norton, 1993.

Pinker, Steven. *The Better Angels of Our Nature: Why Violence Has Declined.* New York: Viking, 2011.

Sayers, Mark. *The Trouble With Paris: Following Jesus in a World of Plastic Promises.* Nashville, Tenn: T. Nelson, 2008.

Schlosser, Eric. *Command and Control: Nuclear Weapons, the Damascus Accident, and the Illusion of Safety.* New York: Penguin, 2013.

Skidelsky, Edward, and Robert Skidelsky. *How Much is Enough?: Money and the Good Lfe.* New York: Other, 2012.

Spitzer, Manfred. *Digitale Demenz: Wie Wir Uns und Unsere Kinder um den Verstand Bringen.* München: Droemer, 2012

Taylor, Charles. *A Secular Age.* Cambridge, Mass: Belknap of Harvard University Press, 2007.

Thompson, Phillip M. *Returning to Reality: Thomas Merton's Wisdom for a Technological World.* Eugene, Oregon: Cascade, 2012.

Verbrugge, Ad. *Staat van Verwarring: Het Offer van Liefde.* Amsterdam: Boom, 2013.

Vogl, Joseph. *The Specter of Capital.* Stanford, California: Stanford University Press, 2014.

Wink, Walter. *The Powers that Be: Theology for a New Millennium.* New York: Doubleday, 1998.

Wright, N. T. *How God Became King: The Forgotten Story of the Gospels.* New York: HarperOne, 2012.

Yancey, Philip. *Soul Survivor: How Thirteen Unlikely Mentors Helped My Faith Survive the Church*. New York: Galilee/Doubleday, 2003.

Printed in Great Britain
by Amazon

80711594R00088